OUR MISSION FIELD IN INDIA

OUR MISSION FIELD IN INDIA

C. V. SHEATSLEY

GYAN

Published by

Gyan Publishing House
5, Ansari Road
Daryaganj, New Delhi-110002
Phone: 011-47034999, 9811692060
E-mail: books@gyanbooks.com

Distribution Network
gyanbooks.com
India, USA, Canada, UK, Australia

ISBN: 978-93-7014-197-1 (PB)

First Published, 1921

2nd Impression 2025

Printed at: Gyan Press, Delhi.

OUR MISSION FIELD IN INDIA
Author: C. V. SHEATSLEY

Our Mission Field in India

THE REPORT

OF

REV. C. V. SHEATSLEY

COMMISSIONER

On the India Field from July 15 to
December 1, 1920

1921

FOREWORD

INFORMATION. This is not an ordinary report. It is the Official Report made to the Board of Foreign Missions of the Joint Synod by the commissioner whom the board sent to India in 1920 to investigate conditions and prepare the way for reconstruction and expansion. The information here given is valuable not only to the board but to all our people. Hence it is published in book form and made accessible to all. The readers of our church papers will be glad to receive such full and intimate information on our field brought down to date.

OPPORTUNITY. Our fifteen years of investigation and discussion and seven years of trial and delay have been followed by an open door and an opportunity far exceeding our expectations. The field that is calling to us for workers and equipment is five times as large as the portion we took over by purchase in 1912. There is no other church body that is now called to carry on the work of the Gospel among the million heathen within this territory. As you read the detailed description of our commissioner, you will be impressed with the fact that the Lord is clearly giving us the command: Go forward!

RESPONSIBILITY. To whom much is given, of him will much be required. Our synod numbers nearly a quarter of a million baptized members. In addition to our extended home mission work, the work of our educational institutions for the training of ministers and Christian leaders, and all our other church work here at home, the Lord has now laid upon us the obligation to carry the Gospel of salvation to a million people groping in the night and the blight of heathenism. Are we equal to the task? That question is answered by the spirit of our response to the other simple question: Shall we fearlessly and faithfully meet the opportunity which the Lord in His providence has given us and the corresponding obligation which He thus lays upon us?

Read and re-read and meditate upon the chapter of "Recommendations." They are not merely the recommendations of our commissioner, but are the resolutions of the Council of our missionaries in India, assembled in consultation with the commissioner. They lay before us a workable program for the near and more remote future. Some of the recommendations are now being carried into effect. Others will be realized according to the largeness of our prayers and the ampleness of our gifts.

Information — Opportunity — Responsibility: Three factors that are vital and indispensable to progress in the work of the Lord. You have them here plainly set before you in their application to our India Mission. May growing interest in the distant field bear fruit an hundredfold in enlarged participation in all our synodical enterprises.

EDWARD PFEIFFER,
President of the Board.

CHAPTER I

General Conditions in India

INDIA, like most countries of the world at the present time, is somewhat in a state of unrest. As we should suppose, she too has been affected by the World War. During the great struggle her native population came into contact with the outside world more perhaps than ever before. Her sons have had glimpses of Western society, civilization, and even barbarism, and, for better or for worse, they have returned to the home-land bearing indelible impressions of what they have seen and heard. Some have become restive and are agitating having their own country become like the great and more democratic nations of the West. Others have turned away in disgust, and are more than ever satisfied with the Hindu religion, the caste, and the civilization of India. Because of these conditions there prevails in all circles certain disturbances that are affecting not only the economic, but also the civil and religious life of the people.

This does not mean that India is in a state of revolution, as the term is usually applied. We may say, however, that a rather quiet transformation is going on, and that gradually India will emerge from the lethargy, and incoherence of the ages and recognize herself, as well as be recognized, as a people capable of greater achievement than has hitherto been thought possible.

True, we do hear of disturbances here and there in the land that are somewhat disquieting, and that would seem to indicate that bloodshed and violence are to be the weapons of an impending overthrow. But these sporadic outbreaks, it seems to us, cannot mean in India what they might mean in a land of more capable and aggressive leadership and more complete organization.

We hear a great deal just now of Mr. Gandhi and his co-revolutionists, with their program of non-cooperation with the government, and their agitation in favor of home-rule for India. While in the abstract this program would be highly revolutionary in a dominion, as for instance Canada, yet we cannot think that in a practical way it will seriously undermine the functions and powers of the government among a people so dependent and patronizing as the average Indian. But the movement must needs be reckoned with, and its ultimate goal, greater freedom or independence, may, in part at least, be attained, since the British government seems to be rather liberally inclined towards her subjects in the India domain. But not only from the Gandhi party but also from more conservative quarters come plans and programs which are meant to urge the Indians to greater self-help, if not to self-government. Out of all this ferment something will ultimately come, even in India; and the missionary must have an open eye and a

Missionary Residence at Tirupati.

steady hand when such threatening movements sweep athwart the land.

But our concern in this report is not primarily with the affairs of the Government, but with the condition of the Christian Church, and more especially, of our own mission work in India. We have mentioned the conditions existing in the state that we may not be surprised when we learn that the same spirit of unrest and revolution is also at work in the Church. An autonomous church is the goal of many aspiring and zealous Indian Christians. In the words of one of our own mission workers: "The Indian Christian Church as a whole is now in a period of transition. Indians are aspiring to have a hand in the administration of the church as an executive body, and to enter into the inner councils of the missionaries; and, therefore, we wish you would not lose any opportunity to train us up so that in the fullness of time Indians and foreigners may do the noble work of the Mission together like brothers."

This aspiration, when moving within proper limitations, is certainly to be commended rather than censured. It indicates that a part, at least, of the purpose of Christian missions is being realized, and that the mission church is to become self-sustaining, and in turn to become a home base for further foreign effort.

We must take account of this waking up. While there is no doubt but that, to some extent, it has been caught up and carried on by the revolutionary whirlwind sweeping 'round the earth, yet like all world movements it has something in it that marks a distinct advancement and should be nurtured and conserved to the up-building and extension of the Lord's kingdom.

How glad we are in the home field when people want to help carry on the work of the Church. How much more should we not rejoice when out in the foreign field hearts and hands are willing, yea eager, to help along? And especially in India, where in the past so very little effort at self-help has come from the native population should we welcome the stir in the leaves as a sign of the Spirit's presence.

We will watch with great interest the trials that are being made of the autonomous church, in both north and south India, especially in the Gossner field of the Lutheran Church in the North and in a Church of England field in the South. Some mistakes will, no doubt, be made; but do we not find that among the most capable, mistakes in policy and administration are often made? Let us not expect perfection among Indians when Europeans and Americans are full of imperfections. Let us be fair.

In a subsequent part of this report we will have occasion to refer to a bit of self-regulation which we in our mission have entrusted to our Indian brethren.

In an economic way India is still very poor. The great mass of her population lives but a few meals removed from famine and starvation, even in fairly prosperous years. About one-fifth of the population,

Church at Puttur.

or 60 million people, lie down hungry every night; and when dread famine stalks in the land, (and there seems to be famine somewhere all the time), its victims perish by the thousands in their hovels or by the wayside.

When going to India I was prepared to meet a poor people, but I was not prepared to see the abject poverty of the average village family. I do not mean that they were all crying for food. In most cases they seemed to have approximately enough to eat, but Oh! the poor primitive condition of the homes and the people. I am sure the entire household furniture and equipment could be bought for less than five dollars, and most Americans could not use any of it at any price. But for ages the people have lived thus and most of them seem quite content thus to continue, for, as they say, "It has been our custom." Sometimes we hardly know whether the universal explanation for everything: "It is our custom," is a bane or a blessing. Bane it is when it stifles progress, effort and initiative; blessing indeed, when it makes people content with conditions that, at best, will require generations of effort to change.

Before I left America some well-meaning and benevolent friends suggested that it might be well to bring a number of the brighter Indian boys to our own country, educate them, and then send them back to their kindred and brethren to work among them and to inspire and help them to higher ideals. I now think this would be a colossal blunder. The foreign educated boys would likely go home and at once express dissatisfaction with their surroundings. They would want different houses, different food, and different clothes, and yet with the means at hand how could these things be provided? The whole procedure would only create trouble and bring greater distress.

We have every reason to believe that with the preaching and teaching of the Gospel among this people the results which will gradually follow will be the laying aside of caste, superstition and idolatry. A new vision of life and death, of things present and things to come, will be gained, and in everything there will be a gradual rising to better conditions and higher aspirations.

It would not do to lift these people suddenly out of their present conditions and place them in a new environment. The people would not know what to do. They would know neither where to begin, nor where to end. They would be like their black ants when a barrier is suddenly placed in their well-worn path. They would at once become utterly confused and run about hysterically until one of them would stumble into the old path again.

It is difficult for us Americans, who have been reared in the machine age, to keep from suggesting or actually installing labor-saving machinery in the place of the primitive, slow, laborious way of doing things. Instead of women grading a railway or wagon roadbed by carrying the ground from an adjoining field in baskets on their heads, we would naturally think a big steam shovel should be installed to make the dirt fly. And in that way, we reason, three men could do the work of three hundred men and women. But then arise the questions: "How will you employ the three hundred? How are they to earn a few cents that they may buy bread?" The answer to these questions at once scraps the greatest labor-saving machine that was ever made for India. For in India, with her over-population and her scarcity of natural resources, work must be made instead of saved.

Providing honorable employment is one of the problems facing practically all Christian missions in India. If the people do not have employment practically all the time, they at once become beggars and public charges. And already there are entirely too many mendicants in the land. In my investigations the most difficult problem with which I had to deal was the economic one. It really baffles solution. In discussing the question with mission leaders and others the end of the matter was usually something like this: "Well, I don't understand how they do it, but somehow the people seem to get along." The multitude, like the one of old, seems to be fed from five loaves and two small fishes. We don't know how it is being done, but the good Lord is doing it every day.

Another condition existing in India that must be constantly reckoned with, especially by the Christian missionary, is *Caste*. Like a baneful disease, it has fastened itself upon the vitals of the country and

Huts of the Outcastes.

must finally eat itself out, we hope, to its own destruction.

Caste may have some slight advantages. One writer says: "It promotes a stationary semi-civilization. It binds together men of the same class. It promotes cleanliness. It is a check in certain directions on moral conduct." But when we examine the counts against the system, it presents a sorry aspect.

An Indian writer, Keshub Chunder Sen, in "An Appeal to Young India," says: "That Hindu caste is a frightful social scourge no one can deny. It has completely and hopelessly wrecked social unity, harmony and happiness, and for centuries it has opposed all social progress. . . . When we view it on moral grounds it appears as a scandal to conscience, and an insult to humanity. . . . Caste is the bulwark of Hindu idolatry and the safeguard of Brahminical priesthood. It is an audacious and sacrilegious violation of God's law and of human brotherhood. It makes civil institutions inviolable divine institutions, and in the name of Holy God sows perpetual discord and enmity among His children. It exalts one section of the people above the rest, and gives the former, under the seal of divine sanction, the monopoly of education, religion and all the advantages of social pre-eminence, and visits them with the arbitrary authority of exercising a tyrannical sway over unfortunate and helpless millions of human souls, trampling them under their feet and holding them in a state of miserable servitude. It sets up the Brahminical order as the vicegerents of the Deity, and stamps the mass of the population as a degraded and unclean race, unworthy of manhood and unfit for heaven."

With the above conditions, agitation for home-rule in the state, the cry in some sections for an autonomous church, the unsatisfactory economic conditions, and the evils of a caste religion, we will have to deal constantly in our mission work in India. They are conditions we cannot ignore; and at the same time we come up against great difficulties in coping with them. However we do not know of any mission field anywhere in the world where formidable obstacles are not encountered in preaching the Gospel of Christ and Him crucified. We should therefore not become faint-hearted when as the ambassadors of Christ we are called to stand face to face with the problems that no man can solve, but meet these problems, sustained by the assurance: "Lo, I am with you alway, even unto the end of the world."

CHAPTER II

Living Conditions

AS already stated in the first chapter of this report the common people in India are very poor, at least when measured by western standards. And by far the greater number of people in India are common people. Aside from a few nabobs, a few rajahs, and some merchants who have possessed themselves of considerable wealth, there are very few rich men among the natives. It might be a good thing that there are but few wealthy people if this meant that the wealth were then generally distributed. But it seems there is not much to distribute. The great mass of the population is always living dangerously near the poverty line.

Nine-tenths of the whole population live in villages of less than 5,000 inhabitants. Four-fifths live in villages under 1,000 inhabitants. The average village in India contains about 365 people. These are mostly small farmers, many of them so burdened with debt that they cannot ever hope to be anything but slaves to the money lenders. These conditions being general, they prevail also in our own mission field.

Let me describe the average Indian village as it is to be found in our mission territory. I should say about nine-tenths of the houses are built of dried mud. Indeed I have been in many villages where every house was of mud and thatched with straw or palm leaves. Streets! there are none; merely crooked roads threading their way among the huts and cattle sheds. Of course there is no water system, except the village well, no sewers and no lights, a very dismal place indeed on a dark, wet night.

But every village has its fine shade trees, perhaps banyans or margosas. Under the spreading branches of these we find the village commons. Here the children play, here the women gather for gossip, and the men sleep during the heat of the day, or talk of their crops in the evening.

As for animals we find a few mongrel curs, some scraggly, poorly bred fowls, sheep and goats; some cattle and buffaloes that should be improved in blood; and a goodly number of crows and some monkeys, with here and there a stray cat. This about makes up the list of visible animal life. Of course there are some snakes, scorpions, spiders, ants, lice; in fact, almost all kinds of vermin may be found hiding in the nooks and crannies.

Let me show you into the average village mud house which serves as a home for the Indian family. It is seldom more than about sixteen feet square and rarely contains more than one room. Frequently there is no window. If there is one, it is not more than a foot or two square with several wooden or iron bars across the opening to keep out thieves. There is never any glass in it. Sometimes there is a real door that may be opened or closed. Often there is

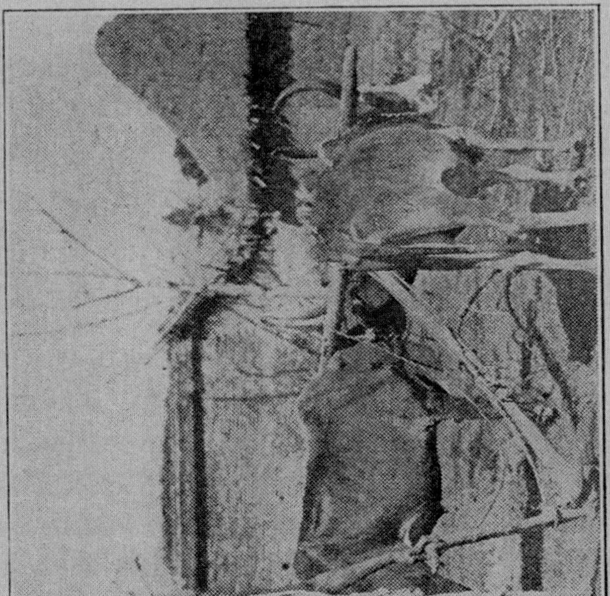

Starting to Plow.

simply a hole through the mud wall for ingress and egress.

The floor is the bare ground with frequently a hollowed-out "paddy" stone sunk in the center. In the bowl of this stone the grain food is pounded before it is cooked. The earthen floor is treated, at least once a week, with a thin wash of cow dung for sanitary purposes. The one room serves not only as kitchen, dining room, bed room and parlor, but the floor serves as chairs, table, and bed as well.

In one corner of the room a little clay is banked up to form a stove on which the clay cooking pots are placed and in which the meals are cooked. There is no chimney. The smoke is allowed to find its own way to the outside with the result that especially when the evening meal is being cooked a smoky haze hangs over the village which seems to come from nowhere or everywhere.

It is remarkable with how few vessels and utensils the Indian housewife can keep house. To the Westerner it is nothing short of marvelous, yet in such a primitive single room hovel a family of eight or ten children will be reared, and after the Indian fashion, successfully, too.

A pole or two across the corner of the room or a mud shelf serve as clothes press. A tiny mirror, a picture of the British royal pair, and a small print or two constitute the adornments of the room.

If the family is a little better-to-do they have a brass water jar and the semblance of a bed, something after the manner of the old trundle-bed with a cord bottom. There is no bedding for it. During the day it is usually edged up in front of the house and serves as drying rack for the few bits of clothing that may have been washed, on any day and at any time. Frequently when the missionary comes the bed is cleared and it is considered a high honor if he will sit on the ropes.

Sometimes the mud is banked up in front of the house under the eaves on each side of the doorway and smoothed off nicely on top and allowed to harden. If the missionary will sit on this bench it is also considered an honor and a blessing to the home. No doubt many a poor soul in India has been brought to Christ by hearing the Gospel preached from this humble seat. Sometimes a strong chest takes the place of the mud bench. In this box all the valuables of the household are placed and the head of the house sleeps on the lid at night. This is for safety's sake. There are no dining tables, dishes, or knives and forks in the village Indian home. Yes, among the Christians there is a small pewter, brass or porcelain bowl for each larger member of the family and one knife for the whole household. The Hindus and Mohammedans eat from tree leaves instead of from plates or bowls. Anything that has been eaten out of once is considered by them unclean thereafter. However they too, always eat with their fingers.

But here! What shall we say to this? In cleaning their teeth they break a twig from the margosa

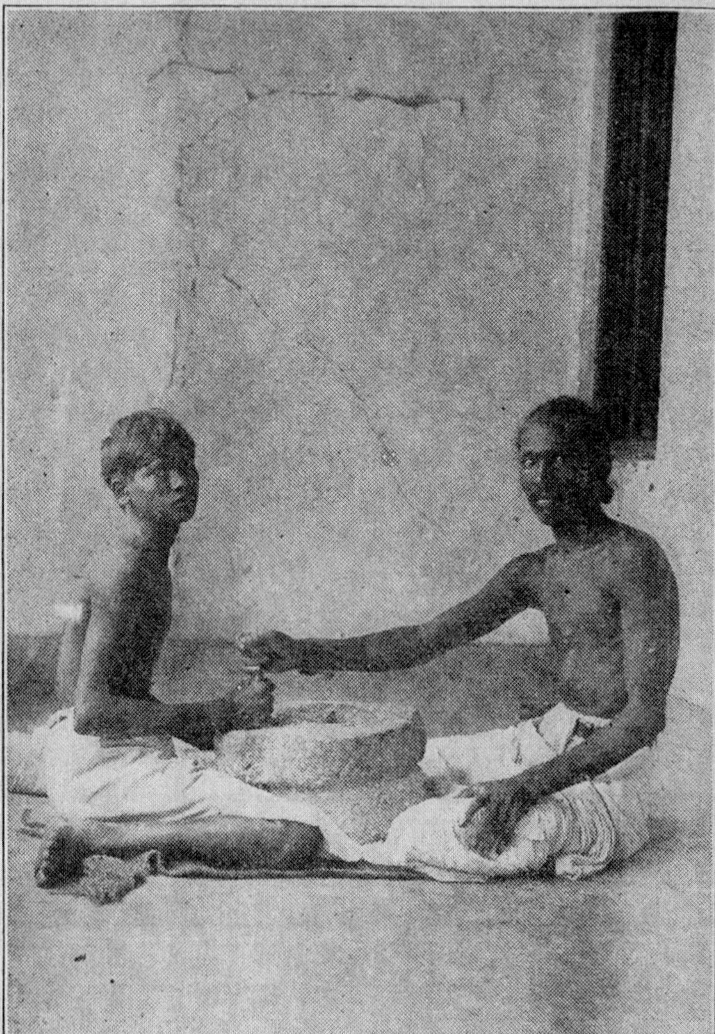

Two Grinding at the Mill.

tree, using the broken and finely slivered end as a brush, and throw it away when they have finished. They think it perfectly filthy that we Westerners use the same tooth brush repeatedly. In answering, I can but think of the German proverb: "Andere Länder andere Sitten."

As for clothing, a few yards of cloth, as it comes from the loom, is all that is needed for men or women. The children frequently go about attired only in a shoe string, sometimes called a "g" string. Even the grown-ups at times seem to have worn their garments down to the last half yard. Let it be said, however, especially of the women, that when they are attired in their usual dress, they are really more becomingly, gracefully and decently dressed than many of our fashionable American women. Some of our women go up and down the streets, not with their clothing worn off by poverty, but cut off, top and bottom, until we should be ashamed to have them appear in Indian society.

The besetting vanity among these people is to wear jewelry. On their wrists and arms, around their necks and ankles, in their ears and noses we see it displayed in various degrees of fineness and loveliness. From beans and buttons, from cheap brass and aluminum up to the finest gold and precious stones runs the scale of value.

One is often surprised how people clad in rags and otherwise poor and needy can afford to carry quite a wealth of jewelry around with them. At a wedding recently a woman of a higher caste handed me her coin necklace for inspection. I almost let it fall because of its sheer weight of gold. Some of this is of the ancient "wealth of Ind'."

Aside from this predilection for jewelry and a certain gaudiness in dress there seems to be little taste for having things fixed up about the home. There are very few flower beds or other ornaments in the yard or garden. In fact, there is usually no yard or garden. Room could likely be found for these home accessories, but there seems to be no taste for them.

Out in the fields they plow with a pair of oxen hitched to a sharp stick, usually iron pointed. And to harrow they hitch to a clumsy wooden rake. For a grain drill they use a little bowl to which they connect three tubes leading down through hollowed wooden shovels. To this apparatus they hitch. The driver puts the grain into the bowl by small handfuls. Indeed, pictures of agricultural implements in use two thousand years ago could be duplicated any day within ten rods of any of our mission compounds.

I might continue to describe the living or economic conditions of this people, but I fear it would take me beyond the scope of this report. I have shown enough, I think, to give you a fair idea of conditions among the people to whom we are called to preach the Gospel. Of course in the larger towns, of which there are a few in our territory, some homes and surroundings are not quite as primitive as those here described, but the great majority are of this type.

Teachers' Residences.

In this connection it should also be noted that many of our native mission workers, such as our teachers and catechists, especially those who live on the mission compounds, have better living conditions and surroundings than the average villager. But we have some workers, and successful ones too, who live right among the people and as the people. Just a short time ago we bought a house and lot for one of our teachers in a village near Rapur for twenty dollars. I mention this to give you the valuation of an average village mud house.

CHAPTER III

Family Life

ONE might suppose that where the surroundings are so very primitive one would find many people roaming about without a home and not caring very much for home life. This is not the case in India. In proportion to the population there are likely fewer waifs and homeless people than in America. The family ties are very strong as well as tender in this land of strange conditions. And while to a stranger it would seem to be a matter of indifference to the native Indian into just which one of the countless hovels he should go for the night, he soon finds that the humblest mud house shelters a family bound together by the tenderest affections. In India as here:

> "Be it ever so humble,
> There's no place like home."

Among Hindus the joint family system prevails almost universally. "It is built on the old patriarchal idea, according to which three generations generally live under the same roof and enjoy a community of life and interest. When a man and a wife have reared a family, the sons bring to the paternal home their wives and live together and raise their families in the common home of their father. The supreme authority rests with the father." Of course to the second generation he has become grandfather, and to the third great-grandfather. He becomes the patriarch of the household. The corresponding mother, while not the head of the house, plays a very important part in the home by having in charge the household food supply.

The entire income of all the members of this usually large family is put into a common treasury, generally presided over by the patriarch or his eldest son or grandson. Out of this common fund all expenses are met. There are no individual property rights. It is really a communistic society or colony. Indeed we might say the arrangement is our family idea extended to the third generation. Many families in America could profit by being a little more like the Hindu household. When children of a few years have become so independent that their parents dare not correct them nor presume to have any jurisdiction over their earnings, it is high time to call a halt, or the family will finally degenerate into a club and the home into a rooming house.

The joint family system has its advantages. It affords family security. It helps a poor people to live economically. "And it has the peculiar merit of developing a strong sense of responsibility in the whole family for its every member, however incapacitated he or she may be for self-support. The weak, the sick and the feeble-minded have the same claim upon the resources of the family as have the others, and the claim is universally recognized. For this reason poor-houses are not needed in India."

In the Cow Pasture.

But there are also defects in this system. One is that those so inclined can become very lazy and still have their daily bread assured. Parasite-like they live from the industry of others, instead of being made to depend on their own efforts. And particularly in India this evil should not be encouraged. Instead of inviting to laziness and inactivity there should be some prodding to initiative and individual effort. More self-reliance should be instilled into the rising generation. Just now there is considerable agitation in this direction, but I fear that because of a lack of training in the past many of those urged to take aggressive and independent steps are not prepared to do so.

There is another defect to the system. Too many live under one roof. Or, if they are not all under one roof, they live in adjoining huts which is nearly as bad. Even seven mild Hindu brothers with their families cannot live together in perfect peace and concord. And, if the brothers should succeed, the daughters-in-law would likely constitute a disturbing factor.

I anticipate that as India awakens to a realization of her capabilities and opportunities the joint family system will gradually disappear.

Nowhere in India did I see parents treat their children cruelly. They always seemed to care for them kindly and even affectionately. And I never saw children treat their parents disrespectfully. Of course I could not understand their language, but the deportment of children towards their parents I could observe. It was uniformly respectful. For example, a Christian or a Hindu boy would never remain seated in the presence of his father. He would rise and remain standing until the father would withdraw or bid the boy be seated. And there was never any "back talk" or smartness displayed toward parents. I often wondered how some of our bright, smart, independent and rudely disrespectful American youngsters would impress the Indian father in a display of this part of their Western culture. He would likely want to protect himself and family against such a civilization.

Children reading this report will likely want to know what the Indian children do during childhood. You may have formed the notion that their life must be very drear amidst their poor surroundings. It is true they do not have the games and playthings usually found among American children. But the great out-of-doors is theirs in India nearly twelve months out of the year. They can go barefooted all the time. And they do, if not from sheer delight, at least by force of circumstance. They can go along to the fields and pastures. They can throw stones to their hearts' content. There is no danger of breaking any glass windows. Do you ask, why? There is no glass in the windows. They can watch the cows and chase the crows, bump their heads and stub their toes. I saw many children engaged in what seemed to be the favorite pastime of chasing the game rooster about the village or starting a dog fight out in the road.

The larger boys take readily to athletics. They play football, barefooted, also Badminton and lawn-tennis. The girls amuse themselves by weaving flowers into their hair or adorning themselves with mock jewelry, or taking care of a real baby, their little brother or sister.

I should not say that the children of India are as cheerful and light-hearted as our American boys and girls. There is a certain sadness and resignation, not only among the children, but it can be seen among the grown-ups as well. It is reflected in practically every thing they do.

I have also noticed a difference between Christian and Hindu children. The former express even in their eyes the hope of their religion, while the latter seem to be rather aimless and without purpose. And this is a reflection of Hinduism.

Marriage among the Indians is the one great event between birth and death. No one intends to be an old bachelor or an old maid. Where these conditions are endured it is because they can not be changed. To go through life unmarried means either a disregard of duty or a visitation from some vengeful god.

Among Hindus the daughter should be betrothed when she is eight or ten years of age. If it is not done then, the parents begin to fear for her marriage. And to have her unmarried amounts practically to a disgrace. Christians do not usually betroth their daughters until they have reached a marriageable age.

In the marriage of the daughter the dowry and not physical charms or accomplishments is the important thing. The amount of the dowry usually determines the grade of husband to be obtained. Sentiment plays no part. Caste and rupees are the considerations. Parents sometimes plunge themselves hopelessly into debt to bring up the dowry in order to pull down the groom. Says Dr. Holland: "The young man and the girl are inspected, and, if both families are satisfied, the betrothal takes place forthwith, and the marriage is not long delayed. The only persons not consulted are the two most concerned, namely, the future husband and wife. To impose implicit faith in one's parents in this matter is the mark of a model son. The bridegroom regards his wife not so much as being his own possession, as an addition to his mothers' staff. 'Where are you going?' asks the mother of her son when he sets forth to fetch his bride. 'I go to bring you a new handmaid,' is the conventional reply."

Unfaithfulness and divorce are not unknown in India. I learned of many cases, even among our Christians, but I do not think these evils are more prevalent than in our own country. The causes also seem to be about the same, infidelity, wilful desertion, and cruelty.

I have heard of polygamous marriages among the Hindus; also the bringing into the home of a co-wife. Statistics show that these evils exist all over the country. Of course among the Christians such marriages are not tolerated.

You will also want to know something as to the prevalence of drunkenness. Do the various members of the household occasionally come home drunk? Yes, I have seen members of both sexes go staggering and babbling home. I have seen them enter into a heated conversation with a palm tree, or upbraid a stray monkey sitting on the compound fence; but, be it said to the credit of the monkey, he was perfectly sober and apparently amused at the antics of his human neighbors.

The chief intoxicating drink, at least in the territory of our mission, is a fermentation of the palmyra tree sap called "toddy." The place where this drink is dispensed is called the "toddy shop." Near our compound at Tirupati is to be found such a joint, and it turns out its product of bleary-eyed, wobbly, loquacious creatures, much after the fashion of the *old* American saloon. I do not think, however, that the evil is as widespread and as destructive as it was with us in the days of the saloon. But its effects are noticeable in many family circles and the missionary will have it to combat.

The aged in the Indian home, largely because of the joint family system, are usually cared for as the circumstances will best allow. Aged parents are practically never to be found alone. Children or near relatives live with them. It does, however, occur that aged people have no home and do not know where

A Tirupati Idol.

to go. This situation prevails, especially among Christians, who, because of their becoming Christian, have been put out of caste by their relatives who have remained heathen, and hence, when age comes on are not cared for in the usual manner. To care for such should be our chief concern. To accept Christ in the face of ostracism and even persecution requires a faith that we should not fail to support in time of need. We should by all means hasten to provide a home for such as these, as well as others among our Christians who are not living after the Hindu fashion, but after the one family system.

Our Christians bury their dead much as we do, though a coffin is seldom used. The graves are sometimes marked with an appropriate stone, but many cannot afford this expense. I did not have the opportunity of attending a funeral service while in India. I saw a number of Hindu funeral processions with their great outlay of ceremony. And I saw one burial near a railway while the train was stopping for water. The dead form was taken from the bier and laid in the shallow grave. The face was covered with a few flowers or leaves, if I could observe correctly. The earth was piled over these remains until it became a little mound by the wayside. In many places the Hindus cremate the bodies of their dead. One can frequently see smoke issuing from the burning *ghat* near the town or village. Near Bombay the Parsees have their "towers of silence," where the bodies of their dead are consigned to the crows and vultures, which, in an incredibly short time, leave nothing but the bare bones.

Poor old India! she has carried millions and millions of her dead to the burning *ghat*, the vultures, or the grave, not knowing that Jesus Christ is the resurrection and the life! How long! O how long! must she wait for the tidings that Jesus her Savior lives?

CHAPTER IV

Morals and Religion

IT might be inferred that because of the very primitive and poor conditions the people would occupy a very low plane of intelligence and be very low in the scale of morals. But we are glad to state that such a conclusion would not be in accordance with the facts.

I have found that the general run of the people in our territory are not dull and incapable of education. On the other hand, they seem to have the necessary brain capacity and a native ability to learn rapidly. They are rather in the position of those who seem not to have had a chance, or as those held down by some great weight. And the millstone is not hard to find. It is caste. "Nothing has ever equalled the satanic ingenuity of this device for keeping permanently submerged the depressed classes of society." And says Rabindranath Tagore: "The regeneration of the Indian people, to my mind, directly and perhaps solely, depends upon the removal of this condition of caste." The burden has, therefore, not been imposed by a foreign ruling power, but the all but intolerable conditions are self-imposed and self-administered.

To be convinced that even the lowest caste people and the outcastes are capable of wonderful development one need but spend a short time with the boys and girls of our schools. Most of these come from the lowest castes and the poorest classes. But their sparkling eyes, alert ears and eager minds do not indicate that there is a dullness or stupidity there that baffles all effort. Many of the youngsters from these schools would lead our American boys of like age a merry chase, for instance, in a language or history examination. Practically every mission in India has its shining examples of scholarship among its Christian workers.

But the general literacy among the people is very low. Dr. J. P. Jones is the authority for the statement that in the Madras Presidency, eighty-five per cent of the male and ninety per cent of the female population are illiterate, and this is higher than the average for India. Surely it will inspire the best of our young men and women to go among the million souls of our mission territory where these conditions prevail and do their utmost to help lift a poor, ignorant and benighted people into the knowledge and glorious heritage of the people of God.

Unless one has lived for a long time among a people, one cannot be sure that his judgment of their morals is correct, and at best, our estimate of another's moral worth can only be approximate. Frequently our estimations are all wrong. I therefore hesitate to say much on the morals of the people among whom I have lived but a few months. But here again I may safely say that Brahminical Hinduism and caste

Hindu Temple at Kalahasti.

have so warped the standards of the decalogue that morality and immorality are hopelessly entangled before the eyes of the people.

Caste says, "Touch defiles, not vicious morals. Of two brothers, the adulterer may live and feed at home; the Christian of blameless character is expelled. A breach of the ten commandments will not exclude a man from caste; but let him drink water touched by a man of a lower caste and he is instantly exiled from society. The following are the most common offenses dealt with by caste tribunals: (1) eating, drinking, or smoking with a member of an inferior caste; (2) killing cows; (3) murder; (4) getting maggots; (5) being beaten by a man of lower caste; (6) abusing or beating relatives held in reverence; (7) following prohibited occupations; (8) breach of caste etiquette, such as leaving a dinner party before others have finished. In the higher castes the offenses now punished are, taking a sea-voyage or dining with one outside the caste." — *Holland.* Nine Hindus out of ten would be more horrified to discover that they had drunk water given them by one of a lower scale than to have been detected in lying or thieving. A person may be known to be a degraded profligate, yet if he has taken certain heathen religious vows he is regarded as a very holy man, and he receives many coins in his begging bowl. A person may tell a bare-faced lie and little, if any, notice will be taken of it; but should one become angry, even on provocation, hands are uplifted in holy horror.

I need scarcely state that such a warped code of morals deflects our Christians also at many points. But here, especially, we must be patient with our people and by precept and example lead them out of this maze and confusion that has been hanging about them and their ancestors for ages.

"India's spiritual history is the world's tragedy of religion. A nation that for so many centuries has sought God with unmeasured sacrifice is still unsatisfied. What is so tragic as the earnestness of unsuccessful search? Here is a people with a limitless capacity for spiritual service and devotion, with a heart hungry for God, that in its real soul has cared and lived for nothing but religion. And yet, for all her religiousness, India is still ignorant of the living God, knowing neither his awful holiness, nor the true glory of His gracious love." —*Holland.*

The Indian is naturally very religious. Everything he does down to the meanest physical labor has, largely because of caste, a religious value or purpose. Natively then we have a religious people among whom to work, and once divested of the dross of heathenism our Telugu Christians could become the counterpart of the early Galilean Christians whom they seem in many ways to resemble. But the Hindus will go on worshipping their countless deities, some of them benevolent, more of them malevolent. They will continue to wander about in their philosophy, their astrology, their superstitions, and in their animism until the light breaks in upon them like the rays of their tropical sun. A learned orientalist says, that "no people has made such efforts as the Hindus to solve, exhaust, comprehend, what is insolvable, inexhaustible, incomprehensible."

CHAPTER V

Women in India

THE condition of its women is the truest test of a people's civilization. Her status is her country's barometer," says Dr. J. P. Jones. If this be true, and in the main I think it is, we can not give India a very high rating. For nearly ninety-nine per cent of her women are illiterate, and a life of drudgery seems to be their predestined lot. At birth already the girl baby is not as welcome as the male child. She enters life with a handicap and it impedes her to the end of her days. Her hope is that in a rebirth she may enter life under more favorable circumstances. In past generations (I am told the practice is nowhere continued now) the mother would send back to the gods the gift that was so unwelcome. This meant that the little girl's life was spirited away, somehow, somewhere. "How foolish! how senseless," you say, "since there can be no sons without mothers." Do what you will, society cannot exist without the fair sex.

In Indian society there are several reasons why the advent of the daughter into the home is not greeted with joy. The first is the prospect of the marriage of the daughter, coming all too soon, with the accompanying heavy cost. "How shall we raise the dowry?" is the anxious question of the parents as one by one

An India Honeymoon.

the daughters come into their home. And be married they must if the whole family is not to be disgraced. And naturally, where the accumulation of a little competence is so difficult, this question of dowry would give considerable concern. There is also the dreaded prospect of girl-widowhood which entails great misery on daughter and parents alike. To have a daughter widowed at eight or ten years, and ostracized from society as well, is anything but cheering to all concerned.

"But human nature is stronger than the iron grip of custom, and the mother-love born with the little child asserts itself after the first disappointment. Although the child does not count for much in the household, the mother is ready to lavish on her those fond endearments which are the lot of babies all the world over. Indeed, in some respects, daughters are in danger of being spoiled. Their parents are very apt to act on the principle, that, as the child at the early age of ten or so must bow her neck under the yoke of her mother-in-law, she should be allowed freedom from irksome rules before that age. So there is, for her, little of that insistence on orderliness, punctuality, strict obedience, and useful habits, such as sewing and tidying up. Left to her own sweet will, she becomes careless and idle, and at the same time precocious."

But it is in place here to state that in the Christian homes of India the daughter is more welcome. Child marriage and the ostracisms heaped upon child-widows are regarded as great wrongs and therefore un-Christian. The hope of all the daughters of India is in Christianity, where there is neither bond nor free, but where all are one in Christ Jesus.

But let it not be understood that woman in the Hindu world has no place and no influence, except that of bearing children and drudging her way through life. "It is true that, apart from her husband and from the kitchen, woman has had few ideals urged upon her in that great country. Her ambitions have not crossed the doorsteps of her house and home. She is measured entirely by her relation to her husband or children. She is her lord's companion and servant. Love to him is the wand which alone can transform her life into gold. Her usefulness and her glory are the reflections of his pleasure and of his satisfaction in her. She has no separate existence. Apart from man she is an absolute non-entity. And yet, within the sphere that has been granted to her, she has shone with a wonderful radiance and with a charm which often reminds us of some of Shakespeare's beautiful womanly creations."

In a religious way, woman in India occupies the same position that she does anywhere else in the world. It is the mother that has the first and best opportunity of impressing her religious feelings and convictions upon the plastic mind and heart of her child. The Indian mother almost unwittingly teaches her child the superstitions and idolatry of Hinduism. There is no systematic religious instruction, but it is, so to say, imbibed with the mother's milk. It is an

Lace School at Gudur.

atmosphere breathed in the home. If Christianity, therefore, is to wield its full influence, the mother must be reached. Access must be had to the home. The Zenana quarters must become the Christian Bible woman's forum. But because of the lack of female education the work of Christian instruction is made very difficult. The barriers of ignorance and superstition can only gradually be broken down. Patience and long continued effort are here cardinal virtues. The Christian teacher must be satisfied if finally a Christian atmosphere has been created where formerly only Hinduism prevailed. But this is already a long step in the direction of breaking up the almost inexorable caste, subservience and superstition that have so long held the women of India in bondage.

The Hindus have a proverb which runs as follows: "Educating woman is like placing a knife in the hands of a monkey." They, of course, mean to say that she not only does not know how to use the equipment, but that it is dangerous for any one to be about when she has this weapon in her hands; or expressed very plainly, keep woman in ignorance. It is where she belongs. Other places in the world than India have given voice to the same doctrine. Not so many generations ago practically the same attitude was taken by our Caucasian progenitors in the forests of Europe.

And we of the Western world who are helping in the great emancipation of women, should also remember that there is another extreme in this business.

When women become so enlightened and advanced that they want out of the kitchen and out of the nursery, and out of the home; when they consider motherhood and home building drudgery and want to do man's work in the counting-house and in the store as well as in the political arena; when women from Christian lands, as we have seen them in India, dress like men, and drink whiskey and smoke cigarettes in public places we fear the emancipation and the "advancement" has been carried entirely too far. It is hardly necessary to state that we do not regard such education as an advancement or an emancipation. This is maleducation. When we speak of the education of woman we mean the preparation that gives her greater strength and influence in her God-given sphere. An education that enlarges her life and beautifies it in the sphere in which she is to move is a blessing of untold value and is not a knife in a monkey's hand. This is the kind of education we mean every woman in India, as well as in America, should have. And I am sure it will ever be the purpose of our mission to exert every effort that woman in India shall have the advantage and blessing of an education that will help her the more easily and effectually to carry the burden and responsibility of her lot. Our hurried opening of the girl's school at Gudur is evidence that we are in earnest in this matter. And we will train Bible women and Zenana workers just as rapidly as our resources will allow.

It is quite plain how Hinduism can thrive with woman in ignorance. Intelligence is not necessary. In fact the system, if a system it is, is unintelligible. Superstition and fear is the only basis needed for practical Hinduism. Intelligence leads away from it, not toward it. The Shastras, the sacred books of Hinduism, have given instruction that no man shall, under penalty of hell, teach to his wife or daughter the Vedas, which are the very best part of Hindu Scriptures. From these references it can be plainly seen that woman under Hinduism is doomed to ignorance. There is no help for her. She must turn her face to Him who said: "Come unto me."

Marriage we have briefly considered under the chapter on "Family Life" so it will not be necessary at this point to say anything further than that child-marriage and child-widowhood go together, the latter naturally following from the former. I shall remember no scene in India more vividly than when I saw a number of these poor children hopelessly, and apparently aimlessly, wandering about. They of course have abodes, but they really have no homes.

"Annually thousands of these poor girls, who are in absolute ignorance of the situation, are converted into virgin widows whose condition, upon the death of their husbands, is instantly changed from one of innocent childhood pleasure into a sad, despised, and hated widowhood. For the parents of the boy sincerely believe that it is her evil star which has killed the boy whose destiny was blended with her own,

Middle School at Puttur.

Thus henceforth she is to be regarded, not only by the parents concerned, but by society in general, as an accursed person, hated for what has happened to her husband, and also a creature to be shunned. Her presence must not be allowed on any festive occasion, lest its evil influence bring sorrow and death to others. Thus a child of four or five years may suddenly have her prospects blasted, her life embittered, and her company shunned by the whole world, with none to befriend, to cheer, or to comfort her. There are two millions of such sad and injured ones in India today. Their cry goes up to God and to man in an inarticulate appeal for relief and redress against a social custom and a religious rule which consigns them, in their time of greatest innocency, to a life which is worse than death itself and which robs them of the protection, love and sympathy which the whole economy of heaven and earth should guarantee to them." —*Jones.*

There is yet another evil that the Hindu religion has inflicted upon the womanhood of India. Many thousands of daughters are dedicated to a life of unutterable shame in connection with the temple worship. These women are known as the "servants of the gods." Out of gratitude to the gods for blessings received mothers give their daughters to this service. It seems to be generally known that all such girls become public characters. Think of the situation! A mother giving her daughter to prostitution as a thank offering to her god. "O religion! what crimes are committed in thy name."

These poor girls are the "dancing girls of India." Everyone knows that they perform certain religious functions and that they at the same time lead immoral lives, but the Hindu religious mind does not balk in having religion and immorality coupled together. A religious man may also be an immoral profligate and yet be in good standing religiously. I have taken time to mention these things in order to show how helpless Hinduism is to bring about a better condition among women as well as among the people of India generally.

The fanatical Hindu will reply, "You have your social evils in America also. You have your divorces and your prostitutes and profligates." And we shall not attempt to deny the all too prevalent truth. And we are also heartily ashamed of these conditions. But they cannot be linked up with Christianity. We have these evils not because of Christianity, but in spite of it. The sad feature of Hinduism is that it has muddled every thing, and is hopelessly entangled. It mixes the moral with the immoral, the good with the bad, the true with the false, until the mind and soul come to the verge of despair.

CHAPTER VI

The Work and Property of the Hermannsburg Mission Society

THE War being over and the German missionaries having been repatriated and their societies dissolved in India, the very difficult problem of what to do with their work and property presented itself. A provision of the Peace Treaty prevented the confiscation of the property as well as the alienation of the work from one faith to another. The clause in the Treaty pertaining to this matter reads as follows: "The Allied and Associated Powers agree that where Christian religious missions were being maintained by German societies or persons in territory belonging to them, or of which the government is entrusted to them in accordance with the present Treaty, the property which these missions or missionary societies possessed, including that of trading societies whose profits were devoted to the support of missions, shall continue to be devoted to Missionary purposes. In order to ensure the due execution of this undertaking the Allied and Associated Governments will hand over such property to boards of trustees appointed by or approved by the Governments and composed of persons holding the faith of the mission whose property is involved."

"The Allied and Associated Governments, while continuing to maintain full control as to the individuals by whom the missions are conducted, will safeguard the interests of such missions."

"Germany, taking note of the above undertaking, agrees to accept all arrangements made or to be made by the Allied or Associated Governments concerned for carrying on the work of the said missions or trading societies and waive all claim on their behalf."

In line with this provision of the Treaty, the British Government in India proceeded to act, and as you will readily recall, your Board proceeded to apply for the work and property of the former Hermannsburg field. All arrangements made during the war for the manning and financing of the work were, of course, to be regarded only as a temporary measure. No permanent claims could be based thereon.

Taking up this work on your behalf in India I soon found that it would be necessary to clear the atmosphere of some misunderstandings, as well as properly introduce ourselves as thoroughly American and capable of caring for a work as large as the Hermannsburg field. It was fortunate that at the time we had enough missionaries on the field to effect a constitutional organization. This at once gave us standing and a certain stability which was so necessary with the authorities as well as among the native Christian workers. The constitution which the India Conference of the Joint Synod adopted lies before you. The entire work would have been jeopardized

Missionary Residence.

had we waited until your Board and the Synod could have approved the constitution. Your commissioner therefore acted under the authority vested in him and sanctioned the constitution for the Board and Synod. I trust his action under these conditions will be approved.

I then interviewed the chairman of the trustees of enemy property in the Madras Presidency, as well as the Government Secretary having enemy missions in charge. Some of these interviews were somewhat lengthy, but I think we succeeded in properly introducing the Joint Synod. Especially in the Government office was it necessary to correct misunderstandings and misinformation. The Government officials informed us that some had even thought that this Ohio Synod or "Ohio Corporation" was simply a body hurriedly organized in America by the Germans for the purpose of covering their missions.

When I told the Secretary that we were chartered in 1849 he was as pleased to receive the information as I was to give it. He also seemed glad to know that we as a Synod stand in no official connection with any European society. To Rev. D. T. M. Leith, chairman of the trustees of enemy property in the Madras Presidency, your Board, I think, owes a vote of thanks. He has most efficiently and carefully handled the difficult and intricate matter of conserving the work of the German missions and at the same time meeting the conditions of the Treaty. Also the missionaries of the United Lutheran Church in India deserve our thanks for their interest and assistance during the trying times of the war and in our negotiations afterwards. I may say here that I found no disposition anywhere among responsible people to destroy or cast aside the Christian work that the German missionaries had by faithful service so carefully built up. Their worth and work was recognized on all sides. But the exigencies of the War and the conditions laid down in the Treaty had to be met.

After many interviews and much consultation with the authorities, I handed a petition to the "Board of Trustees of Enemy Missions" to recommend to the India Government that the entire Hermannsburg work and property be transferred to the Joint Synod of Ohio. The reasons for the appeal were set forth and the assurance given that the work would be faithfully carried forward. The Trustees thereupon reresolved the following: (1) "To recommend that the transfer of the work be approved." (I take it that this clause means that the temporary transfer of the work to our Synod be continued). (2) "To recommend Government to sanction the transfer of the property hitherto belonging to the Hermannsburg Lutheran Mission to the Joint Synod of Ohio to be held in trust for the Church founded by the Hermannsburg Evangelical Lutheran Mission on condition that alienation of the property transferred do not take place without the consent of the Board of Trustees." It yet remains for the India Government to act and the matter will be settled. It is highly probable that the

Government will act favorably since all matters seem to be cleared up and your Board is on the "approved list" of Reference and Counsel in America. The more I consider the recommendations of the trustees the more I appreciate their wisdom and fairness. They recognize and would conserve the work of Hermannsburg. The ultimate goal of Hermannsburg is to be our goal — a self-sustaining and self-administering Indian Church. This is a guarantee and an encouragement to our Indian brethern, a challenge to us, and a tribute to the German brethern. Paul has planted Apollos is to water. We may not arbitrarily alienate the property, yet, in as far as our purpose in possessing it is concerned, we are at liberty to use it as though we possessed it in fee simple.

We are not asked to pay for the property, but are rather to add our efforts to what the Hermannsburg Society has already so unselfishly done for the Church of Jesus Christ in India. Indeed as the whole situation seems to me now it *should* not be otherwise.

All the more heartily and energetically can we enter into the work should it be entrusted to us. And since the Indian Christians on the field have petitioned the Trustees that the property and work be entrusted to us, we can count on their hearty cooperation.

With Kodur and Puttur already in our possession, and our expressed willingness and ability to do the work in the Hermannsburg field, it were a pity if the work were not entrusted to us. It is fortunate that the entire field is kept together. I do not see how we could have built up a successful mission with only Kodur and Puttur as a field, and that bisected by the Tirupati station. The whole field constitutes a block of territory in the heathen world and should be operated as such.

As regards the condition of the properties I may say that general repairs are needed, since during the past five years, very few repairs have been made. It is difficult to estimate the cost of this work, but I think that several thousand dollars will be needed to put the properties in fair shape. If the church at Vacardu is to be rebuilt and several of the others repaired extensively, then six or eight thousand dollars will be needed. I think the Board should make it its policy to put up more substantial school buildings than has hitherto been done, even as a matter of economy. Mud walls or brick laid up in mud, containing no lime or cement, is not permanent construction as you will readily understand.

In the India Conference we planned and took estimates on a standard model village school building; one that in all respects meets the government requirements. It can be constructed, using lime, mortar, and tile roof, for about $200.00 to $250.00. Then we will have a permanent building which does not need to be repaired or rebuilt after every rainy season. Besides the poor condition of the building ofttimes interferes with the work of the school. Sometimes children, on coming to school, find that the building has collapsed during the night. This would all be

Village School.

obviated if we had standard buildings. In general I think it should be our policy to build as substantially as possible. It pays in the long run, especially in India, where climatic conditions are severe. The photographs will give you an idea of the character and construction of the various buildings of the mission. Our missionaries are usually surprised to find the commodious and well-constructed bungalows on the various compounds. This means that our missionaries can go into the various parts of the field and at once begin their work in comfortable quarters. Some may think, on looking at the pictures, that the contrast between the missionary residence and the native houses are too great. Some might think that while we are trying to break down the Hindu caste system we are building up another of Western origin. As a matter of fact our missionaries and their families, reared in the climate and under the living conditions as they exist here in America, could not hold out for any length of time in the native quarters. It has been tried and the results are to be found in the cemeteries of India. Heavy walls and roofs with large, airy rooms and extensive verandas must be provided if the missionary is to remain and do his work.

CHAPTER VII

Inspection of Our Mission Stations

OUR mission field lies entirely within the Madras Presidency, and almost exclusively within the territory of the Telugu language. Roughly speaking, we may say our field begins a few miles north of the city of Madras and extends northward along the Bay of Bengal for a distance of about 90 miles and westward about 75 miles, comprising a territory of about 6,750 square miles, and containing a heathen population of approximately one million souls.

Bounding the territory by mission fields, we may say: It is bounded on the north by the field of the London Society and that of the American Baptists; on the east, of course, by the Bay of Bengal; on the south by the Wesleyan and the Reformed Arcot fields; and on the west by the Arcot field. Our field is rather a remarkable one in this, that on our territory, no other society, Protestant or Roman Catholic, is doing mission work. There is therefore no duplication of Christian effort, although there is plenty of heathen opposition. The fact, however, that here is a field of a million souls that is solely dependent on our efforts to sow the Gospel seed is a challenge for us to do our utmost; a challenge such as we have never before received, at least in the foreign field.

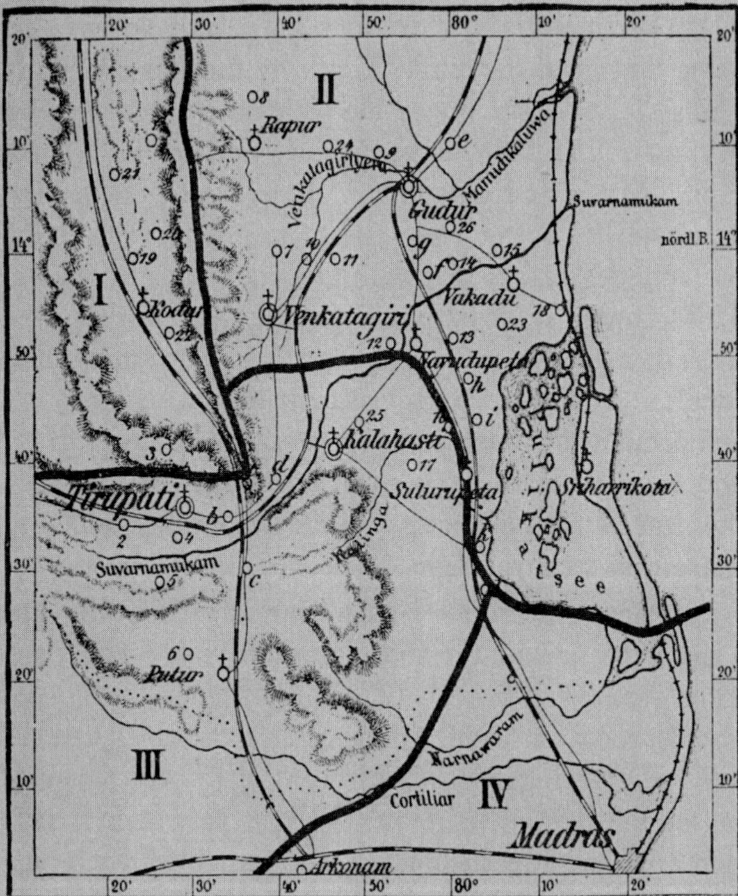

Hermannsburg Mission Territory in Teluguland, India.

♀ Mission Station. ◎ Cities. o Villages. +++++ Canal.

— — Railroads. ——— Highways ..... Southern Border.

Map of Our Mission Field.

The country is in sections quite hilly and rocky, being traversed the entire length by the Eastern ghats (hills). Besides many of the plains are too sandy and dry, as well as salty, to be productive of much vegetation. Much of the land can therefore be designated as waste. Thorny underbrush and cacti seem to be the only vegetation that will take root in many places. This growth, interspersed here and there with a few trees of nobler species and proportions, the natives call jungle. Goats, sheep and cattle find their way through and around this bush and pick a scanty living of grass and leaves. Also snakes, jackals, some members of the deer family, leopards and a few tigers grudgingly share this thorny jungle.

Where water can be had for irrigation we find some very fine and fertile farming land. Here are to be seen waving fields of rice and millet, mango orchards, cocoanut palms and bananas; also fine pastures and vegetable gardens with practically no dormant season throughout the year. Where there is no irrigation or where it is insufficient, the growth of the crops is dependent on the early rains, the south-west monsoon; and on the latter rains, the north-east monsoon. When one or both of these monsoons fail there is dearth and threatening famine in the land. When they fail for two successive years starvation stares many people in the face and relief measures must be taken.

The temperature of this district, I should say, ranges between about 76° and 110° in the shade. During April, May and June on the plains it becomes almost unbearably hot to an American or European. From about the fifteenth of July on one can, by keeping out of the sun, manage to endure the heat without serious results. From October to March the climate is quite pleasant. There is of course no frost and no snow. And our mission boys say the only chance to see ice is to go to Madras where they make it or catch a chance to see it in the refrigerator car of the "Bombay Mail."

In this territory of stony, thorny, as well as good ground our mission field is situated. I will attempt to tell you, somewhat in detail, of the ten main stations of the field as I found them on a tour of inspection. It will not be necessary at this point to describe the properties of each station in detail, as a complete list of grounds and buildings, together with their valuation, is now in the hands of your Board. Recommendations also with reference to the future of the work at the different stations will appear in a subsequent part of this report under the head of "Recommendations."

Puttur

For convenience' sake let us begin with Puttur, our first station after leaving Madras on the Bombay Railway. This is the newest station of the entire field, work having been begun here in 1900.

The mission compound, a short distance from the town, is rather picturesquely situated among the rocky hills. Not far to the south is the "Nagary Nose" a striking nasal promontory on one of the hills. A little to the east is "Lot and his daughters," three rock pillars resembling fossilized giants, especially in the moonlight. Just back of the church on a hill of granite is the poised rock which Brother Nicholson thought he could roll from its pedestal. He went up one day to do the "stunt" but came home reporting the boulder as big as a house. To the west of Puttur is the hill with the hole through it. In the evening with the setting sun back of it, it reminds one of heaven's gates ajar. Indeed the station of Puttur is altogether lovely.

The mission seems to be well situated and in time should become the center of an extensive work. There are 80 villages to be reached from this point. (The number of villages to be reached from each main station I take from a former Hermannsburg report.) At present work is being done at five out-stations. This, however, means that more than five villages are being reached. At the main station, Puttur, there are really three compounds. They give location to a good church building, two missionary bungalows, and a number of teachers' residences, a boy's' hostel, servants' quarters and outbuildings. At present the Nicholsons occupy one bungalow, while the other is used to house the middle school; but this and the boys' hostel are entirely overcrowded. About 130 boys attend school in this building and about 27 are crowded into a hostel that should not accommodate more than 12 or 15.

A Welcome Arch.

There are three primary schools in the village of Puttur, a Tamil school, one for the Telugu boys and a girls' school. A Tamil school is conducted here because it is near the border between the Tamil and the Telugu language areas.

The buildings are in a fair state of preservation, but here, as well as at all the stations of the mission field, rather extensive repairs are needed, since, during the last five years, little was done in this direction. The grounds about the newer bungalow which is now used as a school building, are somewhat shadeless, but steps have already been taken to plant trees. Rev. C. Scriba, resident at Kodur, is the missionary in charge of the work at Puttur.

Tirupati

The next station northward about 23 miles from Puttur is Tirupati. This station, if not quite as picturesque as Puttur, at least has this distinction, that its hills are sacred. As I look up from writing this report I can see the long steep path winding up the sacred hill to the temple of the gods on its crest. And if I take a field glass I can see the weary pilgrims slowly praying their way to the top. I am told that about two thousand pilgrims daily, from all parts of India, climb this hill to the idol shrine at the top; and that the annual offerings made to these gods at this station amount to about $300,000.00. Many of the people come in rags, but they leave their last rupee to win the favor of an imagined deity. Because this place is a "high place" of Hinduism I think there is here a certain fanaticism against everything Christian. But this is all the more reason why we should be on the ground with the Gospel.

We have here practically three compounds, the east, or old compound, which contains the high school, and the west compounds on which are located the church and two good bungalows. The newer of the bungalows, known as the Zenana, we think is the gem of the entire field. It is solidly built in beautiful proportions; and its creamy whiteness against the green background is of most pleasing effect. The older of the bungalows, also of good design and construction is now occupied by Rev. Burger, and Rev. Wilch, and is the bungalow which your commissioner occupied while in that field. It is a sort of general-staff headquarters. A hostel for the Christian boys of the high school is also on these grounds, besides six other residences for teachers, catechists and servants. The buildings, with the exception of those on the high school compound, are in a fairly good state of preservation. There are 320 students in the high school, and repairs and enlargements are necessary. More of this subsequently. The services and afternoon Sunday-school here are conducted either by Mr. Christian, a deacon, or Rev. Burger. About 100 villages are within reach of this station, but there is great need of more aggressive mission work being done. In several of these villages we have schools at the present time.

Missionary Residence at Tirupati.

There is also sufficient ground adjoining Tirupati, belonging to the mission, on which a hospital could be erected, if it is found after a careful survey to be a suitable place for such an institution.

I think Renigunta, a railroad center about six miles from Tirupati, should receive more attention than has hitherto been the case. A neat and substantial chapel is located here and a good school could, no doubt, be established.

Kodur

Going northward about 21 miles from Tirupati we come to Kodur, one of the two stations purchased from the Hermannsburg Society before the War. This station is also situated in a hilly country and has the distinction of having the best climate in the entire mission field; this is principally due to the elevation, it being higher than any other station. Besides the church, mission bungalow and usual buildings of the compound, the lace school has found temporary quarters here and the leper asylum is situated not far from the town. Rev. C. Scriba and his wife have charge of the work, Mrs. Scriba supervising the lace school, while Rev. Scriba looks after the field work and the leper asylum. The institution is located about a mile and a half from Kodur, and is well situated for its purpose, with perhaps the exception, that a river must be forded to reach the place, and during the rainy season this stream becomes somewhat turbulent. The institution grounds contain about 17 acres, part of which is covered with a promising mango orchard. Recently a Government official visited the grounds with the view of possibly locating a large government leper asylum there, and giving us the care of the work. If we can promise a capable doctor we may get the institution. It would be a splendid opportunity to do spiritual work among this most unfortunate class in India. At present there are 11 small buildings on the grounds and 25 leper inmates. Rev. Scriba tells me there are at least 200 of these unfortunates in Kodur and environs, but the great difficulty is to get them to come to the asylum for treatment. This fact I think has prompted the Government to proceed to erect asylums and compel the affiicted to go to them for treatment as well as segregation. The disease seems to be spreading, at least in certain areas.

After our missionaries are located in their respective fields, it would be perhaps better to transfer the lace school back to Gudur, where a separate building has been erected for the purpose, and where, after passing the primary grades, the brighter girls could be taken into the girls' boarding school and the more backward onces could continue at lace work. A good student should not be held back, simply to make lace; while dull and backward pupils should rather be taught lace-making, than continued in their books when little or no progress can be made.

For several years the calls for lace seemed to lag, but now the difficulty is to fill the orders that are coming in. Our good American customers will have to be a little patient and give our lace makers time to catch up. You know making lace by hand is slow work even in America.

At the request of a number of citizens and also at the request of Rev. Scriba a middle school is to be established at Kodur. With the beginning of May next the school is to be in operation. This will give our work an impetus in this place. There is also plenty of room for the extension of the work in this field, especially westward.

Kalahasti

Kalahasti is a very idolatrous looking town, heathen temples and shrines on every hand. And in the town itself we really have no foothold. The mission compound is about three quarters of a mile away, and about three miles from the railway station. The bungalow and church are in faily good repair, the school is very small, having only about seven children in attendance at present. The children from the town cannot be drawn to the school and it is a question whether the school should be taken to the town, since the Government has recently established schools there. But it seems that in some way we must bring the Gospel into this citadel of Hinduism. It remains for the missionary to see how this can best be done. To offset the rather discouraging prospect in Kalahasti itself there is at one of the out-stations, Christamitta, a group of about 80 faithful Christians. They should have a new chapel as soon as possible. Pastor Isaac has been faithfully caring for the Kalahasti field since the removal of the missionaries. With a missionary located at Venkatagiri this station should be cared for until our mission force can be increased, when I think the work at this place should be taken up energetically. It will be difficult, but until we have done our utmost we dare not think of turning aside. There are also many villages in the neighborhood which need school and Gospel work.

Venkatagiri

This rather important rajah seat lies some miles northwest of Kalahasti. The town which is also some distance from the mission compound is of considerable size and importance. There is a very pretty and nicely located bungalow at this place. The church is commodious enough, but is badly in need of a new floor and organ. The school here is also quite small. As at Kalahasti the work is rather far away from the station but none-the-less important. A missionary should be located here as soon as possible. His presence is badly needed. There is a rather productive piece of land in possession of the mission which would afford a good location for an old folks' home and orphans' home. We should have such homes at one of the stations, where especially the wandering aged widows, as well as the homeless children, might find a home. This would be a good place, and the land could be at least partially worked by the inmates to the advantage of the institution as well as to the

Old Chapel at Gudur.

physical well-being of the inmates. A little work is good for the old people also in India.

Gudur

Proceeding northeast from Venkatagiri about 25 miles we come to Gudur, the railway center of the field. This point is easily reached from any point in the mission territory. For this reason it is to become the conference center. Indeed the railway facilities of the field are almost ideal. Within about eight or nine hours every missionary in the territory can be in Gudur.

The material equipment on the compound at Gudur is quite extensive, there being a large church, three bungalows, girls' boarding school, lace school, grade schools and an array of smaller residences and out-buildings. Extensive repairs however are imperative; some of this work is now in progress. Some of the apparently useless and disintegrating compound walls can be removed, others will be repaired. The whole place can be made quite attractive and pleasant. The compound is well located and in time we hope that it may teem with activity and be a great blessing to the entire neighborhood.

It is proposed to re-open the girls' school here about Jan. 1, 1921. Rev. Oberdorfer is to be the missionary in charge of the station, with Miss Laura Nicholson at the head of the girls' school. There are prospects of opening with 20 or 25 girls in the lower classes. It is hoped to eventually develop the school into a high school. It should not be necessary for the girls of the mission, capable of advancing and desiring a high school education, to seek school facilities in other missions.

If the lace school is again located at this place and the girls' school attains the expected proportions the present buildings will not only be completely occupied but some additions will have to be made. If the work prospers the matter of additional buildings here, as well as elsewhere in the mission, will be gladly met.

Rapur

This station lies 22 miles northwest of Gudur and is without rail connections. The highway, however, from Gudur is quite good. There is one river ford, which, during the rains, is difficult of crossing; otherwise there are no difficulties at any time of the year.

A small church, bungalow, school house, and several residences are to be found on the compound. All buildings are rather badly in need of repairs. With reference to the town of Rapur the compound is not well situated, it being practically surrounded by undesirable residence quarters. The town, however, is situated in a fertile valley with a range of wooded hills to the west.

Temporarily at least, the missionary at Gudur can oversee the work at Rapur, with a deacon in residence on the compound. It may be a question as

Missionary Residence at Vacadu.

to whether we should look forward to locating a missionary at this place. Personally, I believe the field could be made extensive enough, and could be developed sufficiently to keep a man busy. There are a number of hopeful villages in the territory. In one village we found all but one family professing Christianity, another village appealed for a school, a third was anxious to have a missionary come to them. There is no other missionary agency at work in the district. We must care for and extend the work. It is ours to do.

Vacadu

Going eastward about 18 miles from Gudur we come to Vacadu, also a station without railway connections. But, like Rapur, it is connected with Gudur or Nayudupet by a good highway, but with a sandy river ford just outside of Vacadu. With the exception of the missionary bungalow the buildings here are badly in need of repair.

The church building has deteriorated to such an extent that it will have to be razed. Divine services are now being held in the bungalow. The whole work from this center needs to be taken up anew. Much of the territory has really never been worked. For example, east of Vacadu about 6 miles is the east coast canal. It is quite an artery of traffic. Many villages lie adjacent to its banks. This canal traverses our territory for a distance of 50 to 60 miles. To my knowledge there is not a single out-station along this entire stretch. It may be found that a missionary with a canal house-boat can do a great and blessed work along this important canal. This method of missionating has been found successful in some of the adjoining missions. We must press east and south of Vacadu, or we may expect that others will go in where we have failed to proceed. I feel certain that aggressive work at Vacadu and environs will show most encouraging results. The bungalow with slight repairs could be made quite habitable. It is one of those places that seems to hold out the challenge that we do our very best.

Nayudupet

Returning to Gudur and going south about 25 miles along the Madras-Calcutta railway we come to Nayudupet, the largest, and in some respects, the most important station of the entire field. In fact in outside circles the entire mission is often referred to as the "Nayudupet Mission." The fame of the Nayudupet brass band has also extended far and wide. For many years this station was the educational and administrative center of the Hermannsburg activities. The compounds and buildings are quite extensive, but here also, repairs are needed.

Besides the commodious church, there are three missionary bungalows, Pastor Punitudu's residence, seminary buildings, book depot, middle school, boys' hostel, industrial department and a number of teachers' residences and out-buildings.

With the beginning of the new year the Seminary is to be re-opened under the direction of Rev. Wilch, assisted by Mr. Gabriel. About 20 students are already enrolled. As soon as feasible the industrial work should again be taken up, and, in general, the old Nayudupet activities should be put in motion. This mission has quite an extensive parish and Pastor Punitudu is kept busy looking after his large flock. But here, as elsewhere, it will take some time until we fully get hold of the work and go forward energetically. When the new regime is well established and our missionaries have grown into the work we may expect to hear of distinct advances and numerical increases in this important center.

Sulurpet

Traveling 20 miles southward from Nayudupet on the same railway line we reach Sulurpet, the last station to be considered in this sketch. It was here, however, that the first work was done by the Hermannsburg Society, and it was to this place that the first missionary — Mylius — came in 1864. Here the Word was first preached among this people of idolatry and superstition.

In connection with this station I must also tell you that repairs are needed. You may tire of the reiteration, but the repairs must be made. School sessions must be held in the church, and one teacher must live in the school because the teacher's house has become uninhabitable.

Deacon Samuel is caring for the work as best he can, but here also I would urge that a missionary be stationed as soon as possible. While Rev. Burger and I were stopping at the bungalow, two Hindu boys, fine looking fellows, came, asking to be baptized. They had formerly studied in one of our mission schools. What a golden opportunity for a missionary. We were told that others were also ready to take the same step. We directed the deacon to these people. He will do what he can, but the missionary is also sorely needed. Here also to the south the ripening fields are waiting.

Rev. Wilch will have temporary charge of this field, but as soon as possible a man should be stationed at Sulurpet. I would not be surprised if in a few years the faithful missionary in this field could report a glorious harvest of souls won for Christ.

Kodai-Kanal

In addition to the above described properties and work we must also say just a word about the rest and recreation station for the missionaries down in the hills of South India at Kodai-Kanal. I did not find time generally to visit this station, but our missionaries who were there in June and a part of July of this past year report that the place is admirably adapted to the intended purpose, namely that of providing a place of rest and recuperation for the tired missionaries during the hottest part of the year. The elevation of the station is about 6000 feet, and the atmos-

Rest Bungalow at Kodai-Kanal.

phere always cool and pleasant. It was a wise provision on the part of the Hermannsburg Society to provide such a refuge for its missionaries. As we have entered into their labors on the plains, so we here enter into their place of rest on the hills. Our missionaries already appreciate this provision. There are four bungalows, with ample grounds surrounding, which may be occupied. But here also some repairs are needed.

Kodai-Kanal has become a great gathering place for missionaries from all parts of India. Various conferences are held during the vacation period, and many subjects of vital importance to mission work are discussed. Time spent at this place is therefore not wasted, but here the missionary and his family gather physical, mental and spiritual strength for a renewed attack upon the strongholds of Satan in the heathen world. The vacation period is usually from four to six weeks in length and is taken during the time of greatest heat from March to June; and is so arranged that not all missionaries are absent from the mission field at the same time.

From this brief survey of the field you will notice that two needs, above all things, confront us; one is a material need, repairs; the other, a spiritual need, missionaries. Say what we will about the new cry of autonomy and self-help in India, the fact remains that, in this field at least, the time for such a step has *not* come. This is recognized, not only by our missionaries, but by practically all the native mission workers. We must first send in our best men and women and put forth our best efforts, then only will the time of self-support and self-direction be brought appreciably nearer than it now is.

The field is our great opportunity and worthy of our very best efforts in Jesus' name.

CHAPTER VIII

Organization of the Forces

YOUR commissioner was not in the India field very long until he was convinced that an immediate organization of the missionaries was imperative, even though there were but few of us in the field and but little actual mission work had as yet been taken up. But it was necessary to organize at once for two reasons: the first, that Rev. Burger, the secretary, was holding everything together as best he could, but was daily waiting for the arrival of the missionaries and the commissioner in order that counsel might be taken as to the best method of procedure. Many difficulties were awaiting adjustment and speedy action had to be taken. Another reason for immediate organization was, that a body petitioning the Government to be given a large mission field in India should have some organization of workers indicating its ability to take hold of a work which had formerly been an organized effort.

Conference of Missionaries

Accordingly we made use of the power vested in us and submitted a constitution and by-laws to the missionaries on July 24th, 1920. After due deliberation the same was adopted with few slight alterations and thus became the governing instrument of the *India Conference*. of the Joint Synod. We trust the Board and Synod found no difficulty in ratifying our action.

As may be seen from a copy of the constitution, regular meetings of the Conference are being held. And from the minutes, copies of which are being sent you from time to time by the secretary, you can see what the Conference is doing and how the work is being carried forward. I would suggest that you carefully preserve these minutes in a separate file for reference, which you may already be doing.

I have no doubt but that with the present organization our brethren in India will be able to carry on the somewhat difficult and intricate work coming into their care. Already, under the direction of Rev. Burger, they have their hands well in the work and are gradually becoming accustomed to handling Indian problems in the Indian way — patiently. I may state parenthetically that I have been rather closely associated with conferences of various kinds during the past twenty years in America, but I am sure our few misionaries in India will have more work to do than any two conferences with which I was associated in this country. They will have in miniature practically all the branches of Christian work as carried on by the Joint Synod in the home field. Their task is no small one by any means. Give them your heartiest assistance.

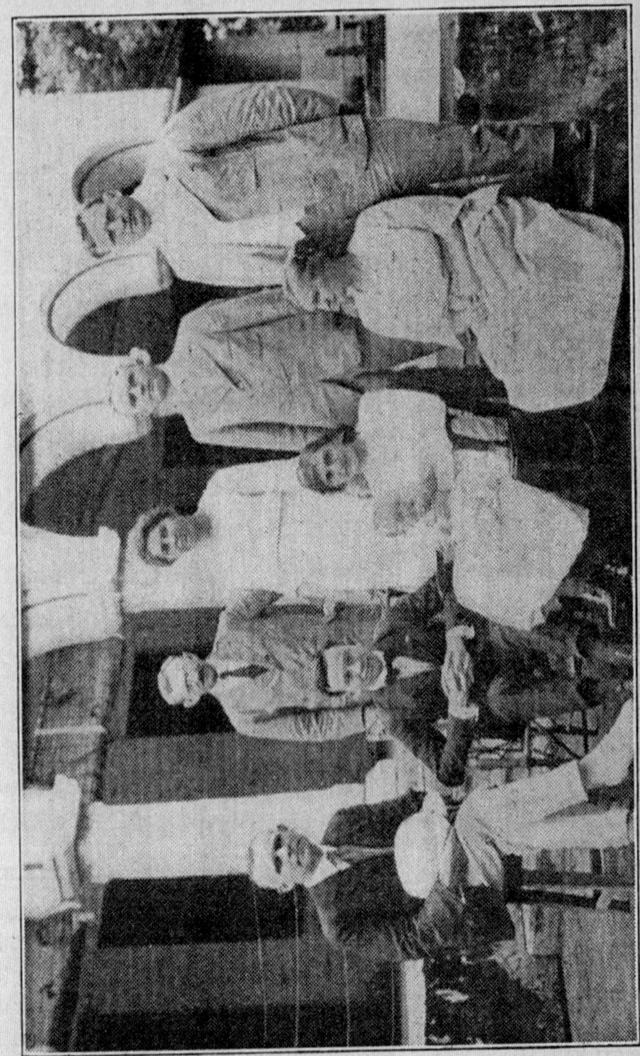

FRONT ROW: Rev. C. V. Sheatsley, Rev. C. Oberdorfer, Baby Ruth, Mrs. C. Oberdorfer, Mrs. E. Nicholson.

BACK ROW: Rev. S C. Burger, Miss Laura Nicholson, Rev. A. Wilch, Rev. Elmer Nicholson.

The India Conference has also forwarded you a copy of "Rules for Missionaries" which we have carefully considered and have submitted to you for adoption. We have not submitted these rules because our missionaries at once became anxious about their furloughs, salaries, allowances, etc., but because we were all on the ground and could study conditions first hand. And since practically the same rules prevail in the United Lutheran Church missions north of us and are the outgrowth of years of experience we deemed it timely to discuss and submit a code of rules for the governance of your missionaries. In the adoption of these rules you will at once have the satisfaction of knowing that they also meet the approval of the men and women in the field. Of course you are at liberty to make any changes you may deem proper.

Conferences with the Native Mission Workers

The arrangement prevailing until this month was that the secretary, Rev. Burger, met the workers, that is, the teachers, catechists, deacons and pastors, in each main station of the old Hermannsburg field, while Rev. Scriba met the workers of the Ohio Stations, Kodur and Puttur, in monthly conferences. Beginning with this month, November, 1920, the Conference secretary, and Rev. Wilch, the treasurer, will assist in holding these conferences. Usually a subject of general interest to the mission is discussed with the workers. Their individual difficulties are laid before the missionary and such other matters as need adjustment are attended to. Not the least among the matters disposed of is paying the workers their monthly salaries. This simple fact always insures a good attendance. No roll need be called nor record of attendance kept, for the missionaries' salary account almost invariably shows that every member was present, unless prevented by serious illness or some dire accident.

When once we have missionaries in all of the stations, then each man will meet his own workers and the conferences can be made more profitable than is possible under the present arrangement. The longer we are here the more we become convinced of the necessity of the missionary keeping in close touch with the workers of his field. The blessing of this we have seen in other mission fields where the work is well in hand. Everything in India, at least all that is Indian, has a tendency to slow down and loll into lassitude, and "let the world turn 'round." I think the average native worker expects to be aroused and started off afresh every once in a while and feels really disappointed if the anticipated prodding does not come at the scheduled time. But remember this, please, that if any of us were to be placed in the position of many of our village mission teachers in India we would also need a mighty strong spiritual stimulant to keep us on the job. Again, the native worker must be dealt with sympathetically and patiently.

Besides the monthly meetings with the workers there is also an annual examination and conference which all missionaries and native workers attend. This meeting is usually held at Nayudupet, at which place it was also held this year. The purpose of the examination is to keep the workers at their studies and make such promotions as the results of the test warrant. The examination questions are prepared by a joint Lutheran Committee in the Telugu country. I will insert here one of these lists, translated into English, so that you may judge to some extent of the work required. Many of the workers fail of promotion and some even are demoted. Of course any one having passed to the grade of pastor is excused from the examination; also deacons who do not desire further training.

Here is the list of questions on Church History submitted to the third class (which is next to the highest) at the annual examination at Nayudupet this year, 1920.

CHURCH HISTORY — CLASS III — TIME, 3 HOURS.

1. Give the history of Jerome and state his qualities.
2. Name books written by St. Augustine.
3. Write in detail their chief purpose.
4. Give date, chief purpose, and result of the Council at Nice.
5. Explain controversy between Chrysostom and Theophilus on the humanity of Christ.
6. Who was Nestorius? What was his false doctrine?
7. Into what countries did the Nestorians spread? What about their condition and number?
8. What evils did the Church undergo due to Mohammed?

9. How did Christianity spread in Europe, by whom, and in what countries?

10. Why did it not spread successfully in Asia?

11. What are the parts of Medieval History? Give dates.

12. What work did Boniface do and what kind of a man was he?

13. What were the three tendencies in the Iconoclastic war?

14. When was the inception of the temporal power of the popes?

15. According to the history you have read this year, of what false doctrines must Indian Christians be careful?

I do not recall that our final examination in Church History at the Seminary in Columbus was stiffer than this one. And I confess I might have difficulty right now in making a passing grade on that list, yet a number of our Indian catechists and deacons evidently passed the test.

Here is a list, not so difficult, for Class I on Biblical History, from the Old Testament.

1. What is the central point of Hannah's song of thanksgiving?

2. What were the deeds performed by Samuel after Saul was anointed king of Israel?

3. What changes came upon Saul after he was anointed king? What morals do you draw from this?

4. What were the words of defiance uttered by Goliath when he saw David? And what was David's reply?

5. On what occasion did David spare Saul's life?

6. Who reproved David, and how?

7. What was the judgment of God over the land of Judah because of the wickedness of Manasseh?

8. What books speak of the destruction of Jerusalem?

9. How were the wisdom and piety of David manifested?

10. What is written in the Old Testament concerning the birth, death, and kingdom of Christ?

These lists will be sufficient to show that our mission together with the other Lutheran Missions of the Telugu area endeavor to maintain a comparatively high standard among the native workers. It shows that effectual work is done somewhere along the line.

The examination conference is always opened with a confessional and communion service. This year the same was conducted by pastors Isaac and Punitudu. It was an impressive service as the company of 130 workers came forward to the Lord's table. It made one feel that this band, thoroughly consecrated, could exert a tremendous force for righteousness in this field. May this indeed be done.

Various business meetings were held. One of these was especially noteworthy where the Indian brethren agreed to relieve the missionaries from the management, handling and responsibility of the funds of these treasuries, viz.: the "Savings Fund," the "Pension and Widow's Fund" and the "Indian Lutheran Mission Fund." This is the first attempt in this mission at self-help, but if the native Christians are ever to take part in the counsels and administration of the Church in their own midst a beginning must be made somewhere. We have begun here. We will watch the experiment with considerable interest. It

Missionary Residence at Puttur.

is possible that in a year hence one or two of the funds will be radically changed or perhaps abolished, but this will not necessarily mean that the administration was a failure. The step was already discussed this year.

At one meeting of the conference two very excellent papers were read and discussed; one on the "History of the Hermannsburg Mission" by Mr. S. Gabriel, and another on "Education in Mission Schools" by Mr. R. Jesudas. Copies of these papers have been presented to the Board.

At another session a very warm welcome was again extended the missionaries and commissioner and a copy of a well thought out appeal, printed on silk cloth and practically addressed to the Joint Synod was handed to your commissioner on behalf of the India brethren by Mr. J. William. A copy of this document is also in the hands of the Board. We of course all responded to the warm welcome and the appeal.

At another time a large children's meeting was held, Rev. Wilch, chairman. Also a very impressive women's meeting was conducted by Miss Nicholson. Sometimes a band concert would be given or vocal selections rendered by the boys of the boarding schools, sometimes in English, at other times in Telugu. All in all the meeting was not unlike an American synodical convention with its attendant services and entertainments. The customary auto ride was missing but in lieu of that we went about in a home-made park-trap drawn by two sturdy oxen.

There was less dust, less noise and fewer infractions of the speed regulations than we ordinarily experienced in America.

When the convention adjourned, I stood at the door and as our Indian workers filed out I grasped each one by the hand, at the same time placing in it a rupee as a token from the Board. This bit of remembrance was highly appreciated, and some indeed, needed the coin in these times of rising prices. 135 rupees were given out; this means that this number of people, besides the missionaries and the young men from the boarding schools were in attendance at the closing session. For comparison's sake we ask, how many more were present when the Joint Synod adjourned at Blue Island this year? I ask the question to give you an idea of the size of our India Mission. What is needed is that the forces be aroused, equipped and directed. Then under the guidance of the Holy Spirit a great work can be developed with the now somewhat dormant forces on the field.

Mission Workers' Salaries

At this point perhaps, better than anywhere else in this report, a word should be said with reference to the pay of the native workers. This was one of the problems hanging fire when we came into the India field. And we found it a most difficult problem too. It is quite likely that we have spent more time and discussion upon this question than upon any other single issue.

It was apparent that in view of the rising prices of food-stuffs in India, especially rice and cotton goods, we would have to advance the salaries of the workers to keep them above the hopeless debt line. We consulted with the missionaries of other missions and found that the same conditions were facing them also. After going over the scale of the salaries, as determined upon or contemplated in other missions about us, our Conference decided to drop all special famine allowances which had been paid the workers during the last few years, and instead add 12 rupees monthly to the salary of each worker. The famine allowance had averaged about 6½ rupees per month per worker. The new scale ranges the salaries from a minimum of 19 to a maximum of 48 rupees per month. Our investigations on the cost of living here lead us to believe, that even with this advance, conditions are barely met. Translated into dollars and cents it means that a family here must live on a salary of from seven to 16 dollars per month. In view of conditions already set forth in this report this is not impossible, but even here, it requires the strictest economy. It should also be stated that many of our workers or members of their families earn something on the side, which also helps in the aggregate. But it is a question whether it would not be better for the mission work to insist that the workers give their entire time to it and pay them higher salaries, rather than have them earn something on the side, and perhaps neglect the work of their calling. Should we also not insist on more efficient work, and pay accordingly, thus finally eliminating the cheap man? These are questions that as the missionaries and Board gain experience can be more adequately met. I may also say in this connection that the salaries now paid our native workers are about on a par with those paid in neighboring missions, although in several missions further increases are contemplated.

It should also be stated that as a further alleviating measure, return fees of boys educated by the mission beyond the high school entrance grade have been reduced to a minimum, provided they then continue in the service of the mission. Boarding school fees have also been reduced and in the case of orphans no fees are charged. These resolutions have not been hastily made nor are they mere outbursts of generosity, but have been reached after much earnest discussion and investigation. We hope the Board will be ready to ratify these conclusions.

CHAPTER IX

The Evangelistic Work

AFTER all, the chief work of the mission is and must remain the direct preaching of the Gospel. This is the first as well as the last duty of the missionary. It is fundamental to all mission work. When this work is lost sight of in a maze of humanitarian efforts and civilizing agencies a mission has ceased to have a distinct message to the heathen world.

It is therefore imperative that the missionary, as soon as possible, learn the language of the people to whom he is to be the Gospel messenger. This our men and women are doing just as rapidly as possible. And they are making considerable progress in their Telugu.

Services in the churches are being held practically every Lord's day. They are conducted either by the native pastors, one of the deacons, or the missionaries, Burger or Scriba. We have attended a number of these services and find they are conducted according to Lutheran forms. I have also been assured that the contents of the sermons were in accord with the Lutheran faith. Of course, I have understood nothing except the Amen. Our native Telugu preachers are not very demonstrative in their preaching. They do not stampede their auditors, like many

After Church at Nayudupet.

of our colored pulpit orators in America. They warm up to their subject, but there is no rant or raving. They use short sentences and simple illustrations. There is scarcely ever any argumentation. They do not develop doctrines, they recite the Gospel. From what I am told I think they should perhaps be a little more pointed in their preaching; a little more "Thou art the man" would help to awaken some of the sluggish sinners. But here, as elsewhere, some of that "mild and gentle" Hindu nature still shows through. Our Telugu folks also like to sing. They like plenty of chanting in the liturgical service and so the Hermannsburg mission made provision for this in its forms of service. I think our missionaries will do well to follow in general the same forms. The great singers among our Telugu brethren are the boys, especially those from the boarding schools. They can sing for hours without tiring, and you should hear them! I wish you all might have the privilege. A dozen of them will create more volume than the average American congregation of several hundred. They simply pour out their young souls in song. They readily sing English melodies, German chorals, or Telugu songs. The boarding boys at Nayudupet, Puttur and Tirupati are especially to be commended for their fine singing. Mr. S. Gabriel of Nayudupet deserves special commendation for his great interest and skill in church music. In fact, Nayudupet is famous in India as the musical center among the Protestant missions. We hope this good reputation may not wane under Ohio direction. Let our Telugu brethren be the singing church among the Christian bodies of India; I am sure Hermannsburg will also rejoice if her efforts in this direction are continued.

As I write this report a petition is handed in by one of the native workers, asking that he may be permitted to sing the Gospel among the Hindus, after the manner of Telugu song they so much like to hear. It is claimed the average villager will listen more attentively if the Bible story is sung or chanted rather than spoken. In an adjoining mission this is done to some extent, with what success I do not know; but several of our workers are enthusiastic for it; in fact they have tried it out, they say, with good effect. Our missionaries will in time be able to judge in the matter. I mention it here because it shows a musical tendency in the people. Personally I have not been able to appreciate the weird, despairing note of the Telugu chanting, but if the natives appreciate it my tastes need not be considered.

Not only in the churches and in the chapels is the Gospel preached, but under the village shade trees or on the street corners and in the homes. Some of the most efficient work is done, when, like the disciples of old, one brother tells another, "We have found the Christ."

There are practically three kinds of evangelistic tours which can be made here almost any time. One kind is that a company of Christians goes out from the mission center to the surrounding villages. This can best be done in the early morning or evening. I have accompanied such a band a number of times on Sunday evenings when the people had come in from the fields. Here at Tirupati the boarding boys usually lead the way into a village, singing a hymn; sometimes they have instrumental accompaniment. As they sing their way to the village commons under the shade trees, a number of people follow them, others gather about, and soon a crowd of men, women and children are ready for the Glad Tidings. Remember that the listeners are practically all heathen. One of the older Christians of the party then begins to relate some Gospel story, and he usually holds the attention until the end. Then another hymn is sung, followed by another short address by one of the Christians, usually of the nature of a personal testimony of the Gospel. Then perhaps another hymn is sung and the more experienced members of the evangelistic party speak personally to some of the listeners; perhaps one will address the children. This personal interview frequently brings out the fact that a number who have listened believe in Christ, but, on account of caste and family ties, are afraid to come out and openly confess His name. They frequently say: "Get the chief men of the village or my brothers and we will all come together." "Cowardly," you say. Yes, in the abstract; but when we remember that the individual who comes out alone to confess Christ will be driven out of his caste, out of his home, out of his village, that his life will be endangered, and in every possible way, his existence made wretched, we can understand his hesitancy. How many of us would be able to stand up bravely for Christ under such ostracism? Again we must be patient with these people and keep on testifying among them. Some fine morning or evening a mass movement will start and a whole village will become Christian, and then perhaps an adjoining village, and so on. Mass movements are not abnormal in India. The people have always moved in the mass or caste-wise. With the natives, religion is above all else social, a matter of the community, the caste. "The village deity was goddess of all the village; together they suffered for her wrath, together they appeased her in sacrifice. If now, Jesus is to be the God instead, He surely must be God of the whole village too." Thus thinks the Hindu, but he seldom acts alone. He moves in the mass. This fact must always be reckoned with in our mission work in this country.

Sometimes in village preaching, a member of the Brahmin caste will break in on the preacher with a question or two, especially if the speaker is antagonizing the gods of Hinduism. But there is no use to argue. You get nowhere. It is best not to antagonize much, but to present the plain simple Gospel.

Another very similar form of evangelistic work is that the missionary, or several of them, together with some native helpers, go on tour, as they say. They take a tent and an entire camp outfit and go to some central location among a group of villages; then

Interior of Church at Nayudupet.

they pray and sing and teach and preach among the people until they have reached the ends of all the villages in the group. Then they pitch their tent farther on until they have made the round of their field. This work is usually done in January and February when the weather is pleasant. This work is productive of much good.

Another way of reaching people with the Gospel is that the missionary or mission worker goes alone to the different homes of the village, and there patiently sits down with the father or the elders and tells and retells the Wonderful Story. The missionary's wife or the Zenana worker can do the same for the women members of the household. This is the slow way of evangelization, but it is not without its lasting effects. The difficulty is that the missionary usually has so many different duties that he cannot find sufficient time to do this work as it should be done. Here is where our native helpers can do much more than is now being done.

It is in a way unfortunate that, as mission work is now carried on in India, the missionary has to be burdened with so very many different things. I say *has* to be burdened, because there does not seem to be much relief in sight, as long as the missionary must direct and account for every little detail. We hope that, in time, at least the business details of the work can be entrusted to other hands. He is practically in the position of the apostles of the early Church who had to neglect the spiritual work to wait on tables.

It seems to me the Indian Archdeacon was about correct when he said to a missionary: "Your control of the purse string gives you a false position, and induces mercenary work. It burdens the spiritual man with a mass of organization; and it blinds the unspiritual man to his own barrenness. For by the power of the purse he keeps going a huge machinery of schools and preachers and out-stations, and never realizes it is but an empty shell. Your work is not to rule but to inspire."

There are many indications that Hinduism is now preparing to make her last stand against Christianity. It has dawned upon the Brahmin, and he is practically Hinduism personified, that Christianity has already made such inroads as to endanger the whole fabric of the religious caste system of which he is the chief administrator as well as beneficiary. Hindu propagandists are going about right here in Tirupati and Puttur stirring up the people against Christianity, telling them that millions and millions of dollars are being raised in America to be sent over here to break down caste. Recently in Puttur our preachers on several occasions have been hooted from the streets of the village because of this agitation.

More than ever, then, the spiritual side of the missionaries' work must be carried forward. India must be reborn in Christ. To this end Christ must be preached. Hinduism has miserably failed, but in her death grapple with Christianity, she can, like the mortally wounded tiger of the jungle, take terrible vengeance. India indeed needs missionaries of every gift, teachers, doctors, nurses, and all the rest, but first and last, she needs the preacher of the Word. She needs the preacher who has time to devote himself to his work. He should have time to listen patiently to the inquirer. He should not seem to be in a hurry.

At this point I would make an observation, which I would not only ask you carefully to note, but which I would submit to all American boards having missions in India. I think most of your missionaries are overburdened with too many duties in addition to their spiritual calling. I fear that the apostolic danger of having to wait on tables instead of preaching the Gospel threatens. In a number of cases I was astounded at what the missionary was expected to do or to look after. He was to be preacher, teacher, evangelist, director, financier, administrator, accountant, builder, peace maker, social leader, member of committees and sub-committees ad infinitum. And all this is to be done in an enervating climate of nearly 100 degrees shade temperature!

My heart went out in deep sympathy to those who wanted to be relieved of some of the routine work and give themselves more to the spiritual side of their calling. The missionaries trained for the pastoral office should have time and strength to devote themselves to their calling. They should be able to give themselves wholly to this work. They should have time to sit down by the well, or on the door step, to

Rev. Punitudu and Family.

stand in the market place, or to go out into the byways and hedges, or to wait for some Brahmin Nicodemus who would come by night. You see what I mean! They need time to preach Christ unto the people, not only indirectly, but directly and constantly. And in most cases I found that this is what their souls yearn to do. Boards! see that your theologically trained men and women are unshackled to do this crying work in the foreign field. Could not consecrated laymen have charge of accounts and building operations? Could they not direct much more of the school work, medical work, etc.? You may reply, "Yes, but all this will take more men and women and more money." True, but more Gospel will be preached and your work will the sooner grow into a spiritual building. When the fields are white unto harvest reaping time has come. Precious time should not then be spent in getting the machinery into shape; or rather, those who are to be chief reapers should not be compelled to sit in the office.

CHAPTER X

The Educational Work

THE problem of educating the masses in India is one of colossal proportions. It will hardly come within the scope of this report to even attempt a discussion of the conditions confronting all education in India, nor yet to lay down plans for meeting the situation. The field is so vast and ramified that any attempt to discuss it would take us far beyond the time at our disposal. Besides, I would not presume to be able to handle this subject after but four months of observation and study. I am glad, however, to be able to refer you to the most recent report of a Commission of Inquiry on "Village Education in India." This report will give you much information which will be valuable to you in helping to direct this very important part of our mission work. That of course which concerns us chiefly at this point is our own educational work in our own mission.

I think our mission territory, as far as literacy is concerned, is about the average of India. This being true the percentage of adult illiteracy is quoted as 89 per cent among men and 99 per cent among women. This clearly indicates that education is sorely needed. Especially our Lutheran Church cannot thrive in ignorance. "We must educate, or we must perish."

We can never hold out against the idolatry and superstition of the heathen world with a constituency that cannot read and write. And when we have succeeded in teaching children to read and write, it is said that in some areas 75 per cent of those who pass through the village schools have to be classed as illiterate ten years later. Dr. Holland is authority for the statement that of the 300,000 Christians in the Telugu area eighty per cent are illiterate. So it is not only a problem of leading the poor natives into literacy but also of keeping them there.

In our area, according to Hermannsburg's report, there are about 2400 villages. Over against this number we do not have a hundred native teachers at the present time, and the number of scholars is perhaps not many more than half the entire number of villages. While it is true there are a number of Government and Hindu schools throughout the district, it is also true that we have the opportunity of establishing schools to the limits of our ability and then not be able to cover the field.

At the present time we have more than enough teachers to man all the schools we have established. I know you will ask, "Then why does not the India Conference send out its spare teachers to establish schools." In the first place, a number of the teachers are not capable and do not have sufficient initiative. The Conference is trying to cull out the inefficient ones. In the second place, a missionary should be on the ground to give encouragement and direction to

Middle School at Nayudupet.

the work. Where this cannot be done the wisdom of establishing schools may be questioned.

As to the curriculum of the elementary schools it goes without saying that reading, writing and arithmetic are the secular basis, perhaps with the addition of nature study, handwork, and music. The "Grant-in-Aid Code" will specify as to these things. As for religious instruction the Madras "Educational Code" says: "Such grants will be given impartially without reference to any religious instruction to all schools which impart sound secular instruction." This means that in addition to the secular instruction religious instruction may be imparted as those establishing the schools may direct. However no compulsion as to the attendance of those not desiring the instruction may be exercised. Of course this is entirely satisfactory to us, as we would not exercise compulsion in religious matters if we had the power to do so. Where no government aid is sought nothing is prescribed as to the curriculum, but I think it is perhaps well to work along with the Government in this matter. It would be very unwise at this juncture of affairs in India not to co-operate with the Government where at all possible in education and in the maintenance of law and order.

As for the middle or secondary and high schools, little need be said at this point as to the curriculum and religious instruction, as these matters can best be arranged by those on the ground in India.

But I think your Board should make it a matter of policy to encourage the more gifted pupils to go on into higher education, not simply with the view of afterwards becoming workers in the mission, but to take up some useful vocation or calling, not directly connected with mission work. I think too many of the Christian boys in these schools have the idea that when they have finished their education they must remain within the walls of some mission compound. They do not seem to realize that if they go out into the world as Christian men they can exert a powerful influence among non-Christians. Their faith does not bind them to caste and ceremonies. They are free. And they should make use of this freedom to release those still held in bondage. Christian lawyers, physicians, artisans and business men, as they go in and out among the heathen, are also missionaries and are doing a great work. I think that this fact needs to be emphasized, especially in our own mission. There is too much inclination to remain a child of the mission when one should be a man in the world. Too many want to sit within the gates when they should go out into the by-ways. Of course in many cases this is not easy because of the ostracism of the Christian in many heathen communities. But this is a cross that can also be borne for Jesus' sake.

As to buildings and equipment for the high school at Tirupati you will find recommendations in the last section of this report.

In regard to the education of the girls of our mission area you will have noticed that our India Conference resolved to re-open the girls' school at Gudur about Jan. 1, 1921. It was only the importance of this work that hurried the Conference to this decision. Besides, some of the girls of our territory were going to other missions for their education, and in some instances, were thus weaned away from their own church. It should also be possible for the young men of the mission, who have had educational advantages to find a wife who has also had some education, within this mission. It is of great advantage, especially where both are able to teach school.

"But any scheme of education for the Indian girl should be based on a wise understanding of the tradition of womanhood into which she is born, of the place she occupies in the life of her own community — and of the functions she is, or may be allowed to perform. The girl is a very busy member of the Indian village home. She draws the water from the well, winnows and pounds the rice, gathers firewood, cleans the house,and in every interval of freedom from these duties carries on the hip the inevitable baby of whose care she is almost entirely ignorant. Besides being maid-of-all-work, she is, as she grows up, a great cause of anxiety to her parents who must arrange for her marriage (not always an easy matter) while she is still a child. These two causes, her home duties and her early marriage, make it very difficult to secure her regular attendance at the village

School at Gudur.

day school. Her attendance at the boarding school is generally more easily secured. This is not surprising when we consider that sometimes the total cost, and almost always the greater part of the cost, not only of instruction, but of maintenance, is defrayed by the missionaries, who also undertake responsibility for the girl's personal safety, thus relieving the parents of a double anxiety."—*Village Education in India.*

Miss Laura Nicholson will have charge, at least temporarily, of our girls' school at Gudur. It is proposed to secure an Anglo-Indian matron who will practically live with the girls in the hostel. They need careful guarding and patient helping, but the work *must* be done. It was thought we could open the school with twenty or twenty-five pupils. We should not have a large number to start with, as we can do better work by finding our way in this (to us) new work.

Perhaps at this point a word should be said with reference to Christian literature. It must ever be kept in mind that the chief purpose of our schools is to help the natives to become intelligent Christian men and women. Every effort in this direction will be in fulfilment of the great Gospel commission. We cannot teach too much Bible. We cannot present the plain way of salvation too often or too completely. But in our presentation we must be careful to keep within the scope of the intelligence of the people. In India, as elsewhere, much that is intended for the edification of the common people fails to edify because it is beyond the grasp of the simple mind. Our missionaries should be urged always to keep this situation before them in their teaching and evangelistic work.

I think it would be a great help to place a set of the large Lutheran Biblical charts in every school with the Scripture text printed in Telugu, and that a generous use be made of the small chart cards with Telugu text and short Gospel story printed on the back, also in Telugu. Such pictures will be studied and texts read and re-read in every literate home. And where parents or children cannot read, the picture will serve in preaching the Gospel.

When one sees what Christian education has done for this poor people one cannot but be anxious that the good work be extended as rapidly as possible. It means a new life and a new hope to "souls in heathen darkness lying." Let us bend every effort in behalf of this blessed work.

CHAPTER XI

The Medical Work

APART from the direct preaching of the Word there is no department of Mission work that affords better opportunities as an evangelizing agency than the medical work. I was profoundly impressed with the importance and opportunities of this work as I watched the sick and unfortunate flock into the hospitals at Guntur, Rajahmundry, Chirala, Rentichintala and Vellore. I thought of the opportunity of pointing the unfortunate to the Great Physician for spiritual help. And I noticed, too, how well the opportunity was being used in practically every case. From the waiting room at the entrance of the hospital to the convalescent quarters the Gospel was presented in word or picture by those in attendance or especially employed for this purpose. Many an unfortunate Hindu or Mohammedan has learned to know and love his Savior during his stay at the Christian hospital. Impressions are made upon him at a time when he is most impressionable. I cannot see how the unselfish work done by the medical missions in India is going to fail to help silence all opposition against Christianity, at least on the part of thinking men and women. I do not see how any one can go away from these Good Samaritan institutions and not be kindly disposed towards those who have so skillfully helped them in their bodily ills, as well as in their soul distress. I have seen in the hospitals at Guntur and Vellore children that had been picked up as poor crippled waifs, that by skillful treatment have been restored to a normal condition and good health. I thought of the power of the Gospel that moved someone in America to go to India and establish a hospital and go out and get a poor, crippled, heathen child and restore it to bodily strength and fill it with spiritual life. How like the Master when He took the children in His arms and blessed them; and how in obedience to His command to go into all the world! Indeed at times it seemed to me that I had been transported back to the time of Christ and that He had just come over from Galilee to India and was now in the midst of the lame, the halt and the blind. And, indeed, the thought is not far from the truth for I saw on the wall the words: "In Jesus' Name." Here were His people doing His work in His name. Oh! how very nigh has the Kingdom come to those who sit in darkness. And many indeed have seen the great Light and have come to the brightness of its rising.

In our mission, those of us on the field are most anxious that we should have a first-class hospital, and a number of dispensaries at the outer stations. We hope and pray that this important branch of our work may soon be inaugurated. A graduate Christian doctor will be needed to start the work. Money

Ten Lepers of Kodur.

will be needed for a hospital. But we do not think that the constituency of our Synod will withhold the requisites for a single moment, once it becomes apparent that the work must be done. If we are going to be faithful to the trust committed to our care we must take hold.

Some of our brethren in America seem to have the idea that all of our missionaries should have some medical training before beginning work in our foreign field. The training, of course, will not come amiss, but medical practice has reached the point, also in India, where the partly trained and uncertified doctor has little or no standing, and cannot prescribe even in urgent cases. Besides, the regular pastor missionary will not have time to practice medicine. His curriculum is already overcrowded.

In pioneer work the situation would be somewhat different. There some medical training would find a practicable field. But even in India, in organized work and in our day, specializing is almost imperative. It would be better for the doctor to be part missionary than for the missionary to be part doctor. We must have medical men and women on the field who are standard in their profession and who are filled with the spirit of Christ. Then we can expect the work to show blessed results. But until we reach this point we cannot expect to do much in medical mission work. We should like to have our medically trained brethren in America know that here we have a field worthy of their best efforts in the medical work as well as worthy of the best efforts as Christian men and women. We hope that the hospital of the Ohio Evangelical Lutheran Mission will soon become a reality, and that it will compare favorably with any hospital of surrounding missions. A hospital and the leper asylum greatly enlarged would give us an equipment for handling most cases of bodily distress that might find their way to us.

I would, in this connection, call your attention to a resolution adopted at the meeting of the National Missionary Council held in Calcutta in November of 1920. The resolution indicates what those familiar with conditions in India think of the work and necessity of medical practice in this land. I append the resolution:

"*Resolved,* That an appeal be made to Home Boards for a large number of nurses and doctors, especially women, to strengthen understaffed mission hospitals and teaching centers, as well as to open up new work in needy rural areas. The Council believes that at the present time medical missions have unique opportunities for presenting the Gospel message to all classes of people, as well as for co-operating with the Government in all matters relating to community welfare."

CHAPTER XII

The Surrounding Missions

ACCORDING to instructions I had intended to visit all the missions of other Churches surrounding our own territory. However, owing to a lack of time, and because of a commission from the National Lutheran Council to visit the Gossner field in the North, I did not get around. In this connection I might add that there is a certain sameness of operation among the missions, so that visiting one or two gives one an idea of the prevailing standards. I was glad to have had the privilege of making a rather extensive survey of the Gossner field; it afforded an opportunity for a study of a people and conditions not quite like the prevailing types in the South. Perhaps therefore the lack of time to visit all the contiguous missions was made up by the opportunity of visiting the Gossner field.

After our own, the Guntur mission of the United Lutheran Church was the first visited. Your commissioner was most heartily welcomed, and every courtesy and opportunity possible was extended him. Here we saw a mission going in full swing, as it were. It was indeed heartening to see what continued, faithful effort in the Gospel could accomplish in a generation or two. Only a prejudiced antagonist of Christianity could fail to see the wonderful transforming power of the Gospel of Jesus Christ, and only an enemy of the Lutheran Church could fail to see the well-balanced efficiency of the Lutheran way of teaching and preaching the Good Tidings. It was certainly encouraging and inspiring to see the hundreds of Indian boys and girls being prepared for their life work under Christian influence. It was a pleasure to address the students of Guntur college and over 300 girls in the Sylvanus Stahl chapel. The medical work of this mission is nothing short of remarkable, especially in the way in which the spiritual welfare of every patient is cared for along with the ailments of the body. It would be a pleasure to describe in detail the extensive work done in this mission, but I must hasten on. Suffice it to say that whether in the college, seminary, medical or Zenana work, girls' school, village schools, printery, carpenter shop, or out in the district, "In Jesus' Name" was always apparent.

What may be said of Guntur may also be said of Rajahmundry, the other extensive center of the United Church in India. At Rajahmundry, your commissioner, as well as all our missionaries, was privileged to attend the Joint Conference of Guntur and Rajahmundry, and to witness the merging of the two missions, which seems to have been successfully and satisfactorily done.

While the work at Rajahmundry is not as extensive as at Guntur it is perhaps in some respects more intensive, and thus the missions working together will supplement each other. When I left

Missionary Residence at Venkatagiri.

Rajahmundry opposition and even persecution on the part of the heathen was developing at some points; at the same time there was evidence of a mass movement in certain districts, twenty-five and thirty converts presenting themselves for Baptism every day.

After a visit of a few days it would be presumption to attempt to criticize. I can only hope that our efforts in our new field may soon become as encouraging as these United Missions.

Early in September I visited the Arcot Mission of the Reformed Church with headquarters at Vellore, just southwest of our field. This mission was founded by the distinguished Scudder family. This family has a record of having given a total of over 800 years of service to the cause of Christian missions. A member of the fourth generation of the family had just come from America, preparatory to taking up the medical mission work. In this mission, as in Guntur, we found the medical branch especially well developed. I must take time to tell you of a line of medical work that especially appealed to me.

On a certain day of the week Dr. Ida Scudder goes out into the country with her automobile, equipped with a dispensary and a staff of Gospel workers. The afflicted and unfortunate, knowing the day of the tour, gather at different points along the way-side under the trees and await the coming of the "Samaritan car." On the arrival of the car the afflicted are led or carried by their friends about the machine where Biblical pictures are shown, the Savior is pointed out as the Great Healer, a hymn is sung, prayer is offered and the bodily ailments treated in a skillful way. The party then hurries to the next group and so on until the afternoon is spent and several hundred heathen have heard the Gospel and have had their bodily ailments treated.

This field of work is practically limitless in India. I hope we may soon have like "Samaritan cars" going out in every direction. I venture these cars would soon supplant the senseless and sensual cars of juggernaut that sally forth on heathen festival days to degrade and crush.

South of our field, I saw something of the work of the Wesleyan Mission. Rev. D. G. M. Leith, at the head of the Kellett Institute, Madras, who did so much for us in our negotiations for the Hermannsburg property, belongs to this mission. I am sure we will all have the highest respect for a mission which counts as its leaders men of the type of Mr. Leith. I also met Dr. Heuman of the Danish Lutheran Church, the Revs. Bexell, J. Sandegren and others of the Swedish Lutheran Church, also Revs. Gulliford and Macphail of the Scottish Free Church, with missions in Madras and vicinity.

To the northeast of our field is the American Baptist Telugu Mission with headquarters at Nellore. I had planned three times to visit this mission but was hindered each time. This mission is in somewhat

Group of Christian Daughters.

close proximity to our own, and there is occasionally a little friction along the border, but our Conference has frowned down on any encroachment from our side. If this same rule will be observed by the Nellore folks there will be no difficulty.

To the north and west of us the London Mission, a Congregational society, has its territory. This field also I did not visit. But I met representatives from all the fields surrounding our territory, and the amicable relations which you desired to have established I think exist at the present time. I do not think that there is a disposition on the part of anyone to encroach upon or hinder our work in any way. On the contrary, I am sure the surrounding missions will extend every courtesy and assistance to our missionaries as they one by one enter the field. In fact this has already been done in a number of instances. Perhaps at this point I may digress enough to say that it was my observation that there was less inclination to a superficial fellowship, and a deeper regard and respect for fellow Christians shown in India than we usually find in America.

Especially noteworthy is the unstinted assistance and valuable counsel given us by the missionaries of the Guntur mission.

This mission has loaned us a Secretary, the Rev. Burger, who has, not only remained on our field in the trying times of the War, but who has made personal sacrifices of such a nature, that, knowing of them, one cannot but appreciate his interest and work in holding the field almost single handed. Dr. McCauly will continue to meet with our Conference after Rev. Burger returns to America for a much needed furlough.

CHAPTER XIII

Recommendations

IN addition to the survey of the work of our mission as presented in the preceding chapters of this report, I would make the following recommendations as meriting your immediate consideration and action. I realize that the program submitted is rather an extensive one and will require considerable man-power and financial outlay from our Synod which is not yet accustomed to extensive work in the foreign field. But we have waited long for such an opportunity, and now that it has come and we have accepted it, it behooves us to fully occupy the field or turn it over to those who will.

Consider that the field has already waited for missionaries for six long years. We must take hold energetically or much of the work done by the former missionaries will have to be done over again. I know that within the Joint Synod the friends and supporters of foreign missions will not want you to stop short of adequately meeting the needs of the field, even if the annual budget must be doubled or even trebled. The Joint Synod with its 146,000 communicant members will surely not consider an average of one dollar per member per year for foreign missions an extravagant contribution. Your appropriation now is but $30,000 per year.

1. In the first place I would recommend that the entire field be manned with missionaries as soon as possible. This will mean the placing of eleven male missionaries in the field, or six in addition to those now there or on the way. Or, divided among the stations, it will mean a man at each of the stations but Rapur, and two men at both Tirupati and Nayudupet, one at the head of the High School and the other at the head of the Seminary. And it might soon become necessary to place two men on the teaching force of the Seminary, and eventually also a missionary at Rapur.

2. That a competent man be placed at the head of the industrial work at Nayudupet.

3. That, if a suitable man can be found for agricultural work, his course be finished at the agricultural college at Coimbatore in order that he may become familiar with India agricultural conditions before beginning the work; and that he study the development of the agricultural work about to be undertaken at Guntur.

4. That if the repairs and new building projects recommended be authorized a man with some architectural knowledge and practical building experience be given charge of all repair and building operations in the mission. Under existing conditions I am sure a competent man would more than save his salary in expediting and economizing the construction.

5. That as soon as feasible arrangements be made to give at least all primary schools such super-

vision as will best serve the interests of pupils and teachers.

6. That a lady principal be placed at the head of the Girls' School at Gudur, relieving Miss Nicholson for nurse work.

7. That a Zenana and Bible teacher have in charge the preparation of native Bible women and Zenana workers.

8. That at least one properly equipped hospital be established within the mission, likely at Tirupati, where we have a suitable piece of land; and that a graduate doctor be placed at the head of the institution with Miss Nicholson as head nurse; and that the Board look forward to the establishment of a second hospital so that there will be one for men and one for women.

9. That a home for aged widows and orphans be opened at Venkatagiri with the local missionary in charge.

10. That the high school at Tirupati be rebuilt and equipped at an approximate cost of $20,000.00 to the Synod.

11. That the entire mission be equipped with the large and small Biblical charts with texts printed in Telugu.

12. That the brass bands at the boys' schools at Puttur, Tirupati and Nayudupet be re-equipped with instruments.

13. That the project of a Joint Lutheran Seminary in India be at least discussed with the Lutheran missions and boards interested.

14. That the request for automobiles by the India Conference be granted, if funds will allow.

15. That the Rev. D. G. M. Leith of the Kellett Institute, Madras, be extended a hearty vote of thanks for the services he has rendered on our behalf in our mission work in the Madras Presidency.

16. That the United Lutheran Church Foreign Board as well as the missionaries, especially the Rev. S. C. Burger, be given a hearty vote of thanks for the interest and assistance they have given us during the trying times of the war and subsequently.

In conclusion I would state that the Lord has been very merciful to me and has granted me exceptionally good health while upon your commission; and while I was reluctant to leave my home and work in America, I am now glad that I followed your call to this very important work. While at times it presented many difficulties and trying situations, it nevertheless afforded a rich experience and an opportunity to do some little work among the great mass of heathen people in the world. For this experience and deepening of my own spiritual life I am profoundly thankful, and I trust that what little I have been enabled to do will help you in directing this important work, and will result in the extension of the kingdom of our Lord.

For your prayers as they followed me around the world I am grateful. I know they have been answered. For the provision you made for my temporal wants and those of my family I thank you. And with all honor and praise to our Lord I herewith cheerfully submit this report for your consideration and action.

(Signed)

C. V. SHEATSLEY.

CONTENTS

ILLUSTRATIONS